STUDENT UNIT GUIDE

NEW EDITION

AQA A2 Business Studies Unit 3
Strategies for Success

Malcolm Surridge

Series editor: John Wolinski

Philip Allan Updates, an imprint of Hodder Education, an Hachette UK company, Market Place, Deddington, Oxfordshire OX15 0SE

Orders
Bookpoint Ltd, 130 Milton Park, Abingdon, Oxfordshire OX14 4SB
tel: 01235 827720
fax: 01235 400454
e-mail: uk.orders@bookpoint.co.uk
Lines are open 9.00 a.m.–5.00 p.m., Monday to Saturday, with a 24-hour message answering service. You can also order through the Philip Allan Updates website: www.philipallan.co.uk

ISBN 978-1-4441-4806-0

First printed 2012
Impression number 5 4
Year 2017 2016 2015 2014

Cover photo: GP/Fotolia

Printed in Dubai

Hachette UK's policy is to use papers that are natural, renewable and recyclable products and made from wood grown in sustainable forests. The logging and manufacturing processes are expected to conform to the environmental regulations of the country of origin.

P01959

Contents

Content Guidance

Questions & Answers

Getting the most from this book

Examiner tips

Advice from the examiner on key points in the text to help you learn and recall unit content, avoid pitfalls, and polish your exam technique in order to boost your grade.

Knowledge check

Rapid-fire questions throughout the Content Guidance section to check your understanding.

Knowledge check answers

1 Turn to the back of the book for the Knowledge check answers.

Summary

Summaries

- Each core topic is rounded off by a bullet-list summary for quick-check reference of what you need to know.

Questions & Answers

Exam-style questions

Examiner comments on the questions
Tips on what you need to do to gain full marks, indicated by the icon ⓔ.

Sample student answers
Practise the questions, then look at the student answers that follow each set of questions.

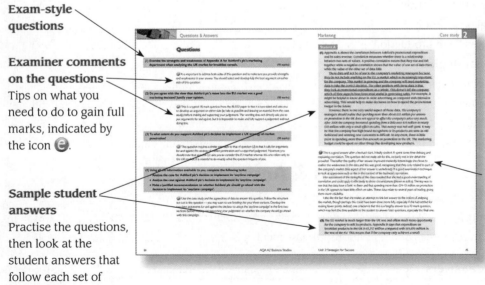

Examiner commentary on sample student answers
Find out how many marks each answer would be awarded in the exam and then read the examiner comments (preceded by the icon ⓔ) following each student answer. Annotations that link back to points made in the student answers show exactly how and where marks are gained or lost.

About this book

This book has been written to provide you with the ideal resource for your revision of AQA A2 Business Studies Unit 3. The book is divided into two sections: Content Guidance and Questions & Answers.

Content Guidance

The Content Guidance section offers concise coverage of the Unit 3 specification. Because the latter contains a large amount of information, this section can only provide an outline of the necessary material, with an overview of the key terms and concepts, as well as an identification of opportunities for you to illustrate the higher-level skills of analysis and evaluation. The scope for linking different topic areas is also shown as this is an important element of tackling this unit successfully.

All areas contain some common elements. Each functional area commences with a consideration of its likely objectives and the external and internal influences that influence these objectives. The following subsections consider these strategies in some detail and how functional performance might be measured. As a result, this unit has a strong numerical base.

Key concepts

Key concepts are shown in bold. You should have a business studies dictionary to hand.

Analysis

In these sections, there are suggestions on how topic areas could lend themselves to analysis. During your course and the revision period you should refer to these opportunities. Test and practise your understanding of the variety of ways in which a logical argument or line of reasoning can be developed.

Evaluation

In these sections, general opportunities for evaluation are highlighted within particular topic areas.

Questions & Answers

The Questions & Answers section is based upon three case studies, which follow the Unit 3 format exactly. Each case study is followed by two sample answers (an A-grade and a lower-quality response) interspersed with examiner comments.

Each case study looks at the functional strategies of an imaginary business that is facing a major decision, and provides numerical and non-numerical information about this business and its market. There are usually four questions contained in each case study, which cover the specification. Broadly speaking, there will be one question on each of marketing, finance and accounts, operations management and people and organisations. The questions carry different mark allocations. One will be worth approximately 10 marks and will test knowledge, application and analysis. Two will be worth approximately 18 marks and will test all examination skills, including evaluation. The same is true of the final question, which has a far higher mark allocation — roughly 34 marks — and requires you to make and support a major strategic decision for the business in the case study.

It is perfectly possible to read the relevant section in the Content Guidance on, say, marketing and then attempt the marketing questions from one or more case studies. However, it is recommended that you attempt all the questions from at least one of these case studies at a single sitting to practise and develop all your examination skills, not least time management. In this case it will be essential to read all of the Content Guidance section before you start writing.

The philosophy of Unit 3

This unit builds on the material covered at AS and examines the ways in which the internal functions of business can contribute to the success of the business through the implementation of appropriate strategies. The unit also considers how the performance of a business might be measured. You will be expected to gain an understanding of the internal operations in the context of larger businesses as well as a broad understanding of strategy. You should also aim to develop the ability to:
- use knowledge selectively to judge the performance of a business
- develop arguments on how to improve the business's performance
- take decisions, identify and solve problems using knowledge of the internal functions of the business

The examination

The Unit 3 examination is based on a case study plus three or four appendices of data. The examination lasts 1 hour 45 minutes and has a mark allocation of 80. It is worth 25% of the marks for the entire A-level (50% of A2). The sample examination papers that are included in the final section of this book give you a clear indication as to the structure and content of the Unit 3 examination.

The case study

This will be about 700–800 words. It will give some background on an imaginary business as well as information on the operation of the various functions of the business — marketing, finance and so on. The case is likely to provide you with some detail about a strategic decision that the business has to take in the near future. Examples of this could include launching a new product, relocating the business or investing in retraining the workforce.

The case study will be supplemented by some appendices of data. These will relate to the functional areas of the business and could cover topics such as:
- market share, size and growth rates
- number of businesses in the market and change in market prices over recent years
- data relating to revenue, costs, profits and cash flow

- operations data such as a critical path diagram, comparative production costs and investment in research and development
- other data may relate to the human relations function of the business. This could include productivity figures and data relating to employer–employee relations (days lost to strikes for example)

The questions

The examination will normally include four questions, three of which will require evaluation. A typical pattern of questions might be as follows:

- A single question which requires analysis, but not evaluation. This might have a mark allocation of 10 and could be a calculation.
- Two evaluation questions based on particular functions of the business, such as operations management. These questions will consider aspects of the business's strategies in these areas and will have a tariff of approximately 18 marks.
- A final question with a tariff of over 30 marks inviting you to assess a particular functional strategy that the business is considering. Depending on the wording of this question, you will probably need to consider the case for and against adopting the particular strategy and to provide a justified recommendation of whether or not the business should go ahead with it.

This final question will have a major influence on the mark you receive for Unit 3 and will be a significant determinant of whether you attain an A* grade for business studies. You must allow sufficient time to plan and write your answer to this question fully. It should be the final question you tackle, as you may draw on earlier answers in support of your views.

Content Guidance

Functional objectives and strategies

Corporate and functional objectives

Corporate objectives

Corporate objectives are the overall goals of a whole business. Corporate goals vary according to the size and history of the organisation.

A business's corporate objectives could include the following:
- growth — to increase the overall scale of the business
- diversification — looking to sell new products in new markets
- achieving the maximum possible profits in the long term
- developing innovative goods and services

The setting and communication of clear corporate objectives helps senior managers to delegate authority to more junior employees while maintaining the organisation's overall sense of direction.

Figure 1 Relationship between functional and corporate objectives

Functional objectives

A **functional objective** is a goal pursued by particular functions within a business, such as human resources or marketing.

A functional objective is likely to have a numerical element and a stated timescale. The achievement of such objectives by the various functional areas of a business will contribute to the success of the business as a whole in achieving its corporate objectives. The relationship between functional and corporate objectives is shown in Figure 1 on page 8.

Relationship between functional objectives and strategies

A **functional strategy** is the medium- to long-term plan used by a business function to achieve its functional objectives.

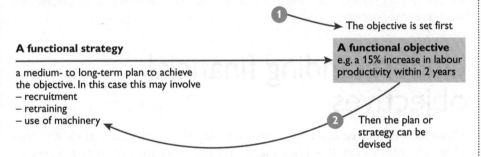

A functional strategy

a medium- to long-term plan to achieve the objective. In this case this may involve
– recruitment
– retraining
– use of machinery

① The objective is set first

A functional objective
e.g. a 15% increase in labour productivity within 2 years

② Then the plan or strategy can be devised

Figure 2 Functional objectives and functional strategies

The functional objective should therefore be set first (and should contribute to the attainment of corporate objectives) and then the strategy should be devised in order to achieve it (see Figure 2).

Analysis

Considering why a business might have set a particular functional objective and the advantages and disadvantages of this objective offers an opportunity for analysis. The reasons for this decision might include reducing costs to improve profit margins or operating in a more environmentally friendly way, especially if the waste is toxic or harmful.

Evaluation

Opportunities for evaluation in this area include:
- Judging whether an objective is appropriate for a specific business in its particular circumstances.
- Assessing the likelihood of the business achieving the objective.

Examiner tip
Do look for evidence of the business's functional objectives in the BUSS3 examination case study. This can be used to justify any decisions you may make about the business's future actions and decisions.

Knowledge check 1
Using examples, explain the difference between an objective and a strategy.

Links

There are endless possibilities for links in this area of the specification. The achievement of one functional objective can have considerable consequences for other functions within a business. Suppose a company wishes to increase its profit margins — an objective set by the finance department. This has implications for all other functions. HR and operations, for instance, may be expected to reduce costs as part of the strategy; marketing may be required to increase sales and/or prices, and so on.

Financial strategies and accounts

This section examines the financial objectives of larger businesses, the ways in which financial performance might be measured and the financial strategies that businesses may deploy.

Understanding financial objectives

A **financial objective** is a target pursued by the finance department (or function) within an organisation. It is likely that a financial objective will contain a specific numerical element and also a timescale within which it is to be achieved. There are a number of financial objectives that a business might pursue.

Cash flow targets

Cash flow is the money flowing into and out of a business. For many businesses cash flow is vital to their success. Banks, for example, require a steady inflow of cash from depositors; without it, they do not have the necessary funds to take advantage of profitable lending opportunities.

Other organisations whose financial objectives centre on cash flow may include growing businesses that need regular inflows of cash to finance the purchase of increasing quantities of items such as labour and raw materials.

Cost minimisation

A financial strategy of **cost minimisation** entails seeking to reduce all the costs of production that a business incurs as part of its trading activities to the lowest possible level. In the case of the budget airlines, for example, this has extended to minimising labour and administrative costs by using the internet for booking.

Examiner tip
Cash flow targets are more likely to be relevant for businesses with a long cash cycle such as house builders, but may have limited value to other businesses such as supermarkets which operate with shorter cash cycles. Thinking about the relevance of particular financial targets for businesses in examination case studies is an important part of writing evaluatively.

Having a financial objective of cost minimisation has clear implications for the objectives (and hence strategies) of other functional areas within a business. Unless managers of all areas aim to minimise their own expenditure, it will be difficult to fulfil the objective.

Return on capital employed (ROCE) targets

The **return on capital employed** (commonly referred to as ROCE) is calculated by expressing the net profit made by a business as a percentage of the value of the capital employed in the business.

A business might set itself a ROCE target of 25%. This means that its net profit for the financial year will be 25% of the capital employed in the business. This financial objective has the advantage of being relatively simple to measure. To achieve such an objective can require actions to increase net profits as well as to minimise the value of assets used within the business.

Knowledge check 2

Why might shareholders support the adoption of a return on capital employed (ROCE) target?

Shareholders' returns

Some writers say shareholders' returns are the current share price and any associated dividends that are due in the near future. Others take a longer-term view and define shareholders' returns as a combination of short-term returns (both share prices and dividends) and future share prices and dividends.

Increasing shareholders' returns requires the support of functions other than finance within the business. Minimising costs is often an important element of the strategy and, as we saw above, this can have significant consequences for all parts of a business.

Internal and external influences on financial objectives

Internal factors

Internal factors arise within the business.

- **The corporate objectives of the business.** Arguably this is the most important influence on any of a business's financial objectives, since the whole point of a financial objective is to assist the business in achieving its overall corporate objectives.
- **The nature of the product that is sold.** For example, if the demand for a product is sensitive to price (i.e. if the product is price elastic), managers may well be more willing to implement and pursue cost minimisation as a financial objective.
- **The attitudes and aspirations of the business's senior managers.** If the managers of the business hold large numbers of shares (perhaps as part of a share option scheme or as a result of founding the business), then increasing the shareholders' value might be an attractive financial objective, especially if a long-run view is taken.

External factors

- **The actions of the business's competitors.** It is unlikely that a business will ignore the behaviour of its competitors when setting its financial objectives.
- **The availability of external finance.** If a business is experiencing difficulty in raising capital, financial objectives are more likely to centre on profits and profitability.
- **The state of the market.** If the market for the business's products is expanding, it may lead managers to set more expansive financial objectives such as higher rates of shareholder returns or higher figures for ROCE.

Examiner tip
Remember that other stakeholders might influence a business's financial objectives.

Figure 3 shows how financial objectives are subject to influences from inside and outside the organisation.

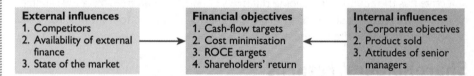

Figure 3 Financial objectives are subject to influences from inside and outside the organisation

Analysis

This is likely to centre on arguing the implications — both benefits and drawbacks — for a business of adopting a particular financial objective. A second area for analysis is to consider the major influences on a business's decision regarding the adoption of a specific financial objective. You may want to think about the relative importance of internal and external factors.

Evaluation

Opportunities for evaluation in this area include:

- Whether the adoption of a specific financial objective is likely to prove beneficial to a business — this will entail weighing up the potential advantages and disadvantages.
- Whether internal or external factors have been the major influence on a business's decision to adopt a financial strategy. Alternatively you may want to identify what is the major factor influencing this decision.

Links

As with the previous section, there are endless possibilities for links in this topic. For example, a financial objective of cost minimisation will affect all other functions within the business as they will be expected to reduce their costs too. This applies throughout much of Unit 3. It is important that you think about links as you study and revise, as this will help you to write more developed responses to examination questions.

Using financial data to measure and assess performance

Structure and contents of balance sheets

The **balance sheet** (see Figure 4) is an accounting statement of the firm's assets and liabilities on the last day of an accounting period. The balance sheet lists the assets that the firm owns and sets these against the balancing liabilities — the claims of those individuals or organisations that provided the funds to acquire the assets.

Assets

Assets are categorised as non-current assets and current assets, while liabilities may be listed as capital, non-current liabilities and current liabilities.
- Non-current assets are those assets such as machinery, equipment and vehicles that are bought for long-term use (generally taken to be more than a year) rather than for resale.
- Current assets are items such as inventories and raw materials and unsold goods, receivables, money in the bank and cash. All of these current assets will be converted into cash by the end of the financial year.

Liabilities

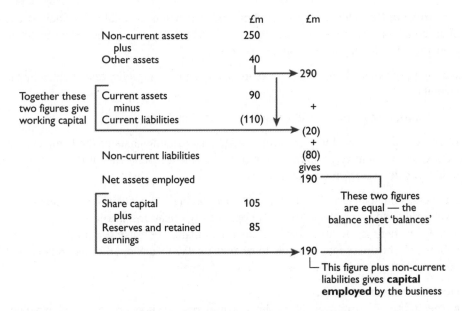

Figure 4 Structure of the balance sheet

A business's assets will automatically be matched by its liabilities, as explained below.
- Shareholders' equity or total equity is the money invested in a company by shareholders in order to acquire the assets that the business needs to trade. It is a liability because the business technically owes it to the investors.

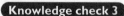

Knowledge check 3

Classify each of the following as current assets, non-current assets, current liabilities or non-current liabilities: a) cash in the business's bank account; b) an overdraft; c) a 12-year bank loan; d) debts owed to a supplier; e) the business's property; f) goods made but not sold.

- Non-current liabilities are moneys employed in the business that have been borrowed from external sources which will be repaid over the 'long term' (a period longer than 1 year). Examples include mortgages, bank loans and debentures.
- Current liabilities are debts of the business that will be repaid in the 'short term' (less than 1 year). The most common current liabilities are payables and bank overdrafts.

The assets owned by a business are financed by its liabilities. If all the assets of the business are listed on one side of the balance sheet and all the liabilities of the business are listed on the other, the two totals should balance.

How to analyse balance sheets

There are a number of important issues relating to balance sheets.
- A balance sheet is just a 'snapshot' on one day of the year. If interested parties are examining the accounts several months in the future, the information may be totally out of date.
- The assumption is often made that because a company possesses thousands or millions of pounds worth of assets, it is doing well. However, the key issue is *how* the company has financed the purchasing of these assets. If it has borrowed heavily and a rise in interest rates occurs, a business may face severe problems.
- External considerations must also be examined, such as the state of the market or economy and similar-sized organisations in the same industry.

Balance sheets, working capital and liquidity

Working capital refers to the amount of funds a firm has available for its day-to-day operations — the liquid assets, in other words. **Liquidity** means the extent to which a business is able to pay its short-term debts.

Working capital is an important measure of a business's liquidity and is given by the formula:

working capital = current assets – current liabilities

Working capital is used to pay for the day-to-day running costs of the firm, such as wages, and to finance the purchasing of replacement inventories. It is also used to fund any sales made on credit terms.

Knowledge check 4

Why is it important for a business to have the 'right' amount of working capital?

Businesses must ensure that they do not have too many current assets in the form of inventories and receivables (that is, people or organisations who owe the business money). If there is too little working capital available, because too much is held by debtors, the business may struggle to finance its day-to-day operations and may not be able to afford to purchase new non-current assets.

Liquidity measures two factors:
- The ability of a firm to meet its short-term debts, as suppliers' bills and expenses can only be paid with cash. Liquidity in this sense measures the company's cash or near-cash equivalents as against short-term debts.
- The ability of a business to turn its assets into cash. Cash or near-cash equivalents (e.g. bank deposits and receivables) are termed **liquid assets**. Assets that are difficult to turn into cash (e.g. buildings, machinery) are termed **illiquid assets**.

Balance sheets and depreciation

Non-current assets have a limited life, even though this could be decades in the case of buildings and some machinery. Instead of charging the full cost of an asset to the year in which it is bought, it is usual to charge some of the cost to each year of the asset's life. This appears as a charge on the income statement and the process is termed **depreciation**.

There are several possible causes of depreciation:
- **wear and tear** — through use the asset eventually wears out
- **obsolescence** — eventually a machine will be replaced by faster, more efficient models, though the old machine is still in perfect working order
- **time** — some assets, such as patents or leases, have a set legal lifetime and therefore lose value as time passes

When assets are depreciated each year, the amount of the depreciation is included on the income statement as an expense. This means that the amount of the business's profits may be reduced.

> **Knowledge check 5**
>
> If a business increases the amount of depreciation that is included within its accounts, what would be the effect on its profits, assuming no other changes?

Structure and contents of income statements and how to analyse them

Structure of income statements

Income statements were previously called profit and loss accounts. An **income statement** is an accounting statement that shows a firm's sales revenue generated over a trading period and all costs incurred in earning that revenue. Making a profit is a significant business objective.

Structure of an income statement

	(£ million)
Revenue	41,000
Cost of sales	(36,500)
Gross profit	**4,500**
Expenses	(750)
One-off items	(150)
Operating profit	**3,600**
Finance income	300
Finance costs	(250)
Profit before tax	**3,650**
Taxation	(1,000)
Profit for the year	**2,650**

In simple terms, an income statement measures the level of profit made by the organisation. In accounting terms, the word 'profit' on its own has little meaning. Profit is such an integral objective and such a good indicator of company performance that it is broken down into two main types.

(i) Gross profit. Gross profit is the measure of the difference between sales revenue and the cost of manufacturing or purchasing the products that have been sold.

$$gross\ profit = sales\ revenue - cost\ of\ goods\ sold$$

Gross profit is calculated without taking into account costs that could be classified as expenses (e.g. administration, advertising) or overheads (e.g. rent, rates).

(ii) Operating profit. After calculating gross profit, the next stage is to remove all other expenses and overheads (those costs which are not directly concerned with the trading activities of the business). The result is net profit.

$$operating\ profit = gross\ profit - (expenses + overheads)$$

Again, operating profit is a very useful measure. A business may find itself making a very healthy gross profit but a very small operating profit in comparison to its competitors. This may be because its overheads are not under control.

(iii) Finance income and finance expenses. The former relates to interest that the business receives on accounts that it holds with banks and other financial institutions. The latter is the interest that it pays on loans. Financing costs can add to or subtract from a business's operating profit.

(iv) Profit before and after taxation. Companies pay corporation tax on profits. At the time of writing, the rate of corporation tax paid by larger companies is 28%. Tax is deducted to give profit after taxation for the year.

Analysing income statements

Profit quality measures whether or not an individual profit source will continue. A company may make one-off profits from the sale of assets, but these may not be a sustainable source of profits and, if so, will be termed low-quality profits. On the other hand, a company with a strong trading position, which can be expected to make profits in future years, is described as generating high-quality profits.

Companies may use profit in two main ways:
- **Retained profits.** These are the share of profits kept by the company and added to the company's balance sheet reserves. Retained profits increase the value of the company, so helping it to expand.
- **Distributed profits.** These are the portion of a company's profit shared out to external parties, such as owners or partners, preference shareholders and ordinary shareholders.

Assessing the strengths and weaknesses of financial data in judging performance

There are a number of issues that you may need to consider when assessing the value of financial data in judging the performance of a business.

Importance of comparisons

It is normally very difficult to make a judgement about a business's balance sheet or income statement without having something to compare it with. There are two main possibilities.

Examiner tip

Profit quality can be an important line of argument in an answer. If an income statement makes reference to one-off items that contribute to profits, it may be that the quality is poor (as it is unlikely to be sustainable) and this could be an important point to develop.

- The performance of the same business in previous years. It is helpful to compare the profits or net assets employed with the business for the year before and preferably for several years previously.
- The performance of similar businesses. When making judgements, it is helpful to look at key figures for other, similar-sized businesses and those that operate in the same industries or markets.

Judging performance against stated objectives

This gives you a yardstick against which to make judgements on the financial performance of a business. If, for example, a business has an objective of growth, it may be reasonable to expect lower profits as it invests more in promotion, research and development and possibly in reducing prices to increase sales.

Window dressing of accounts

Window dressing is presenting company accounts in a way that seems to enhance the financial position of the company. It involves making modest adjustments to sales, debtors and inventories when preparing end-of-year financial reports. In many cases, window dressing is simply a matter of making minor changes to the accounts and is not misleading.

Important methods of window dressing are as follows:
- **Massaging profit figures.** Surprisingly, it is possible to 'adjust' a business's cost and revenue figures. Following a poor year's trading, a firm might inflate its revenue in the final month of trading by moving sales forward from a later period.
- **Hiding a deteriorating liquidity position.** This allows businesses to improve the look of their balance sheets. For example, a company may carry out a sale-and-leaseback deal just prior to accounts being published. This increases the amount of cash in the business and makes it look a more attractive proposition for potential investors.
- **Boosting asset values.** Particularly in the area of intangible assets, such as brand valuations, companies can state the value of these items as being considerably more than their actual worth.

Analysis

This section of the specification has a lot of potential for questions which require analysis. In general, you may be asked to consider whether a business has performed well over a given trading period, using information from the balance sheet and/or the income statement. You may be asked to use this evidence to argue whether a business should take out further loans or raise capital in other ways. Other questions may require you to use the business's position with regard to working capital or profit quality to support the case for or against particular functional strategies.

Evaluation

There are also significant opportunities for evaluation in this area. These include:
- Judging whether a business's financial performance is strong enough to support a particular financial (or other functional) strategy. For example, a business

> **Examiner tip**
> When analysing financial data in an examination, try to link them to other information in the case study. You may have information about the performance of rival businesses, the company's financial (or other) objectives, or market trends. Using this information can help to develop arguments and to justify your judgements.

may be considering a major investment in new products and you may be asked to assess the viability of this strategy in financial terms using evidence from balance sheets and income statements.

- Assessing whether a business's financial performance has improved over a period of time. This is likely to involve analysing the trend of its performance and taking into account factors such as profit quality and window dressing.
- Making a judgement about the value of financial data when assessing the performance of a specific business in particular circumstances.

Links

Once again there is rich potential in this area for links between topics within Unit 3. Any major functional strategy is likely to have substantial financial implications. These can operate at two levels.

First, the business will almost certainly have to raise capital to finance the strategy, and financial documents will help you to assess whether it can afford this and how the capital may be raised (through loans or shares, for example). Second, balance sheets and income statements can be important sources of information when assessing the impact of previous strategies. Have they increased revenue and the value of the business, for example?

Interpreting published accounts

Examiner tip
You are given all the necessary ratio formulae as part of the Unit 3 examination paper; you do not need to memorise them. It is important, however, to know which ratios to use in given circumstances.

The focus here is on calculating ratios, but more importantly on:
- selecting the right ratios for a given situation
- interpreting the results of your ratio calculations
- understanding their implications for business decision making

Ratio analysis is a technique for analysing a business's financial performance by comparing one piece of accounting information with another. Ratios may be used by:
- managers, to monitor the performance of the business
- shareholders and potential shareholders, to assess likely risk and returns on investment
- suppliers, to assess the likelihood of receiving payment and whether to offer credit
- employees, to determine the extent of future pay claims
- competitors, to benchmark their own performance against that of the firm in question

Ratios can be classified according to type. They can be used to assess the following aspects of a business's operation:
- profitability
- financial efficiency
- liquidity and gearing
- shareholders' ratios

Profitability ratios

For many businesses in the private sector, profit is an important measure of success. Profit can, however, be measured by use of several different ratios.

Net profit margin

This ratio measures the relationship between the net profit (profit made after all other expenses have been deducted) and the level of turnover or sales made.

$$\text{net profit margin} = \frac{\text{net profit}}{\text{revenue (sales)}} \times 100 \text{ (expressed as a percentage)}$$

The higher the percentage, the better. This ratio establishes whether the firm has been efficient in controlling its costs.

Return on capital employed (ROCE)

This is an important ratio — also called the 'primary ratio'. It measures the efficiency of the business in using its capital to generate profits.

$$\text{ROCE} = \frac{\text{operating profit}}{\text{total capital employed}} \times 100 \text{ (expressed as a percentage)}$$

Total capital employed is the sum of total equity plus non-current liabilities.

The higher the figure for ROCE, the better. To assess the ROCE figure for a firm, it should be compared with:
- the business's ROCE figures for previous years
- the ROCE for other companies
- the current rate of interest

Financial efficiency

Financial efficiency may be measured using the following ratios.

Asset turnover

This ratio measures a business's sales in relation to the assets used to generate these sales.

$$\text{asset turnover} = \frac{\text{revenue}}{\text{net assets employed}}$$

In other words, this formula measures the efficiency with which businesses use their assets.

Interpreting the ratio:
- An increasing ratio over time generally indicates that the firm is operating with greater efficiency.
- A fall in the ratio can be caused by a decline in sales or an increase in assets employed.
- The results of asset turnover ratios vary enormously. A supermarket may have a high figure as it has relatively few assets in relation to sales. An engineering firm is likely to have a much lower ratio because it requires many more assets.

Examiner tip
The net profit margin ratio is a part of the AS specification and will not be included in the list of formulae provided in the examination paper. However, you can use this ratio in your answer, if you wish.

Examiner tip
Profit margin figures achieved can vary according to the business's circumstances and the industry in which it operates. Do not argue that a low figure is always bad; for example, a business with an objective of growth may cut prices, thereby reducing its profit margin (but achieving increased sales).

Knowledge check 6
Why might a business's managers be particularly interested in inventory turnover?

Inventory turnover

Inventories used to be called stock. This ratio measures the number of times in 1 year that a business turns over its inventory of goods for sale.

$$\text{inventory turnover} = \frac{\text{cost of goods sold}}{\text{average inventories}} \text{ (expressed as however many } times)$$

$$\text{where average inventories} = \frac{(\text{opening inventories} + \text{closing inventories})}{2}$$

Interpreting the ratio:

- This ratio can only really be interpreted with knowledge of the industry in which the firm operates.
- A greengrocer, for example, is likely to turn over inventories virtually every day, as goods have to be fresh. Therefore, you would expect to see a result for inventory turnover of approximately 250–300 times per year.
- A second-hand car sales business would possibly expect to turn over its entire inventories of cars and replace with new ones about once every 2 months. Therefore you would see a result of approximately six times.

It is possible to convert this ratio from showing the number of times an organisation turns over its inventories to showing the average number of days inventories are held.

$$\text{inventory turnover} = \frac{\text{average inventories} \times 365}{\text{cost of goods sold}} \text{ (expressed as } days)$$

Receivables' collection period

Customers who are granted credit are referred to as 'trade receivables'. Trade receivables used to be called debtors. This ratio shows how long, on average, it takes the company to collect debts owed by customers.

$$\text{receivables' collection period} = \frac{\text{receivables} \times 365}{\text{revenue}} \text{ (expressed as } days)$$

Interpreting this ratio:

- Different industries allow different amounts of time for receivables to settle invoices. Standard credit terms are usually for 30, 60, 90 and 120 days.
- The receivables' collection period figure should therefore be compared against the official number of days the organisation allows for settlement.
- For this ratio, the shorter the receivables' collection period, the better.

Payables' collection period

Trade payables used to be called creditors. This ratio shows how long, on average, it takes the company to pay its suppliers. Businesses benefit from a stronger cash position if they are able to delay payment to suppliers, but this action may result in the loss of goodwill from suppliers.

$$\text{payables' collection period} = \frac{\text{payables} \times 365}{\text{cost of goods sold}} \text{ (expressed as } days)$$

Interpreting this ratio:

- Different industries allow different amounts of time for payables to settle invoices.
- The answer may depend on (and reflect) the balance of power between the business and its suppliers.

Knowledge check 7

What is the difference between profitability and financial efficiency?

Examiner tip

It can be very useful to compare trade receivables' and payables' collection figures. If a company takes longer to collect its debts (receivables) than to pay its suppliers, it may face cash problems.

Liquidity (including gearing)

Liquidity is the proportion of a business's assets held in a form easily convertible into cash. Thus a firm is liquid if it holds a high proportion of liquid assets such as cash and debtors. Liquidity measures a business's ability to pay its debts on time. Firms seek to hold sufficient liquid assets to ensure that they can fulfil their financial commitments, but not too many since liquid assets earn low returns, if any. Liquidity can also be termed solvency.

Liquidity can be measured using the current and acid test ratios.

Current ratio

current ratio = current assets : current liabilities

A general convention is that a business should operate with a current ratio of 2:1. This means that it has £2 of short-term assets for every £1 of short-term liabilities. This means that it should not encounter a liquidity crisis. However, many modern businesses operate successfully with much lower figures for the current ratio and also the acid test ratio, discussed below.

Acid test ratio

acid test = liquid assets (current assets – inventories) : current liabilities

A 'normal' figure for the acid test ratio might be between 0.6:1 and 1.1:1, depending on the type of business.

Gearing

Gearing is quite often classed as one of the liquidity ratios as it focuses on the long-term financial stability of an organisation. It measures the proportion of capital employed by the business that is provided by long-term lenders against the proportion that has been invested by the owners. The gearing ratio shows how risky an investment a company is by showing how much of an organisation's capital has been financed by debt.

$$\text{gearing} = \frac{\text{non-current liabilities}}{\text{total capital employed}} \times 100$$

Capital employed is the sum of total equity and non-current liabilities. If non-current liabilities (or long-term loans) represent more than 50% of total capital employed, the company is highly geared and may represent a high risk to investors.

Shareholders' ratios

Shareholders are mainly concerned with assessing their expected returns from investing in a particular company.

Dividend per share (DPS)

This ratio is the total dividend declared by a company divided by the number of shares the business has issued.

Knowledge check 8

Why might the acid test ratio be considered a better measure of a company's liquidity than the current ratio?

Examiner tip

Some ratios can be more important than others in responding to examination questions. Acid test (or current ratio), ROCE and gearing give you measures of a business's short- and long-term financial position as well as its profitability.

$$\text{dividend per share} = \frac{\text{total dividends}}{\text{number of issued shares}}$$

The results of this ratio are expressed as a number of pence per share and a higher figure is generally favoured, although some shareholders may prefer a lower DPS if greater returns and a rising share price occur in the future.

Dividend yield

This is the dividend per share (for the entire year) expressed as a percentage of the market price of the share.

$$\text{dividend yield} = \frac{\text{dividend per share}}{\text{market share price}} \times 100$$

Again, shareholders favour higher figures, preferably exceeding the rate of interest.

Figure 5 summarises the various types of ratios discussed above.

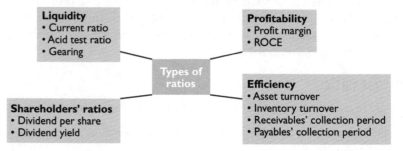

Figure 5 Types of ratios

Assessing the value and limitations of ratio analysis

Ratio analysis is a helpful tool in analysing the published accounts of a business. Rather than considering a single figure, such as operating profits, using ratios enables you to compare the figure against something else, such as the value of capital available to the business. This allows you to make more informed judgements about performance.

Ratios are also applicable to all the vital aspects of a business's financial performance — not just its profitability, but also its liquidity, whether it has borrowed too much and whether it is efficient. Ratio analysis can thus enable all of a business's stakeholders — managers, shareholders, payables, suppliers and customers — to make informed judgements.

However, although ratio analysis is a powerful tool, it does have several drawbacks:
- It is **retrospective** — it concentrates on past performance and is not forward looking. Changes in factors such as the external environment mean that an analysis of a firm's history may not prove to be a good guide to future performance.
- **Different companies may use different accounting policies**, making true comparison difficult.
- It provides **no information about non-financial matters**, such as the state of the market, the morale of the workforce or the experience of the management team.

- It **does not take into account the effect inflation may have** on reported figures, especially sales.
- It is difficult to **compare like with like** — finding two companies that are exactly the same in terms of size, product mix and objectives is almost impossible.

Analysis

The name 'ratio analysis' suggests that there is much potential in this topic for questions asking you to analyse data. The key point here is that not only should you be able to carry out the appropriate calculation, but you should also be able to comment on the meaning of the results. You should make sure that you know what is a 'good' result for each ratio, and how the definition of 'good' might vary according to the types of business and market.

More specific lines of analysis could include the following:
- Analysing the forecast impact of a particular strategic decision on profits.
- Examining the liquidity position of a business.
- Explaining the effects of a particular decision on shareholders.

Evaluation

Possible lines for evaluation include:
- Assessing whether a business can afford to implement a specific functional strategy.
- Evaluating the best way for a business to raise capital.
- Considering a business's financial efficiency.
- Judging the value of ratio analysis in specific circumstances.

Links

Possible links to other areas include:
- the firm's product portfolio
- the state of the economy — especially the trade cycle
- the management style and human resource plans of the business
- the business's corporate objectives

Selecting financial strategies

A **financial strategy** is a medium- to long-term plan designed to achieve the objectives of the finance function or department of a business.

Raising finance

A business has to consider the way in which it will raise the capital it needs to finance functional strategies such as relocation or developing new products. There are three major approaches to raising finance.
- **Borrowing.** Some businesses may raise substantial sums by borrowing from banks or other financial institutions. This is relatively simple to arrange, especially

> **Examiner tip**
> When tackling questions on the value of ratio analysis, you should look for information that may tell you about the future prospects of the business, which ratio analysis will not reveal. For example, is the market growing, is the company launching new innovative products?

if the business has non-current assets that can be used as collateral against the loan. This strategy for raising finance commits the business to regular interest payments, which may mean that borrowing is less attractive to businesses that are not profitable or have cash flow problems.

- **Selling shares.** Alternatively managers may choose to sell shares in the business. This is a slower approach and can be relatively expensive. It can also be a difficult proposition at certain times if the business's share price is declining. In addition, it may dilute the control that a particular group of shareholders has over the organisation. However, it does not commit the company to regular interest payments. Instead the managers will be expected to pay a share of the profits to the shareholders.
- **Other sources of finance.** Some organisations may be in the fortunate position of holding non-current assets or holdings in other companies that can be sold to raise funds for investment in the business. This is an ideal means of raising finance in that it avoids any sort of payment.

Knowledge check 9

How might ratio analysis assist a business when deciding how to raise its capital?

Implementing profit centres

A **profit centre** is an area, department, division or branch of an organisation that is allowed to control itself separately from the larger organisation. It makes its own decisions, following corporate objectives, and produces its own income statements for amalgamation with the rest of the business. A business might find this an attractive financial strategy for a number of reasons.

- Allocating costs and profits on a specific area basis allows for more accurate decision making.
- Monitoring of budgets, targets and performance is much easier with smaller areas.
- Decentralised decision making allows areas to make decisions faster and be more responsive to changes in local conditions.
- Delegated power and authority to profit centres improve motivation.

A wide range of businesses use profit centres. British Airways operates most of its routes as profit centres and Starbucks restaurants are organised as profit centres. However, there are a number of disadvantages from the use of profit centres.

- Profit centre allocation can cause rivalry between centres, resulting in them competing with other profit centres rather than with other businesses.
- Individual centres can become too narrowly focused and lose sight of overall business objectives.
- Communication between centres can become difficult and slow.
- Coordinating the activities of many small areas is complex.
- Performance of individual areas may be adversely or favourably affected by local conditions, making analysis and comparison difficult.
- The allocation of costs can be complicated, expensive and inaccurate. Costs can act as a de-motivator if managers do not take ownership of them because they feel they have been imposed (e.g. company administration costs).

Examiner tip

Do spend some time mastering profit centres as this is a topic on which students often appear unsure.

Cost minimisation

This can be classified as a financial strategy as well as a financial objective. Businesses will seek to implement a cost minimisation strategy by implementing a number of possible policies.

- **Minimising labour costs.** This may be important for firms supplying services, as many of them are likely to face wage and salary expenses which are a high proportion of total costs.
- **Relocating.** Moving to Eastern Europe or Asia will assist in reducing labour costs and also overheads such as property costs. However, in the case of manufacturing, the cost advantages may be offset to some extent by increased transport costs.
- **Using technology.** Technology can replace expensive staff for businesses located in high labour cost countries such as the UK. For example, low-cost airlines rely heavily on the internet to process bookings for flights.

A strategy of cost minimisation has significant implications for all functional areas of the business. For example, the marketing department will have to develop a marketing strategy based on a low-cost, low-price product.

Knowledge check 10

Why might cost minimisation be a more effective strategy when demand is price elastic?

Allocating capital expenditure

Capital expenditure is spending on new non-current assets such as property, machinery or vehicles. Businesses only have access to a limited amount of capital, and any expenditure decisions normally have significant opportunity costs.

- **Investing in machinery.** Businesses may opt to do this to reduce the amount of labour used and the associated costs. This approach will involve heavy initial expenditure on capital items but may lead to a reduction in spending at a later stage. It also offers the potential advantage of increasing the productivity of the business. There are drawbacks, however. The initial costs are high and workers may need retraining in order to operate the technology efficiently.
- **Investing in property.** Some businesses invest heavily in property to enable them to trade effectively or possibly to support their corporate image. Thus supermarkets in the UK hold a huge portfolio of property in high-street and out-of-town locations, as they would be unable to operate without it. Allocating capital expenditure in this way can help a business to attain its overall corporate objectives.

Analysis

You should be able to argue the strengths and weaknesses of particular financial strategies in given circumstances. To help you do this, you should consider the benefits and drawbacks of each of the listed strategies as you study it. In addition, you should be able to analyse the implications of a particular financial strategy for all functions within a business.

Evaluation

There are also opportunities for evaluation in this area, including:
- Judging the best strategy for a given business in specific circumstances and supporting this judgement.
- Assessing whether a chosen strategy is likely to be successful on the basis of financial and other information that is provided.

Making investment decisions

It is important to appreciate that even the safest investment is not risk free. Firms use a series of techniques to forecast costs and likely returns and to judge these figures, taking into account non-financial factors too.

Firms can forecast future earnings arising from an investment with more certainty if:
- the market is stable and sales forecasting is relatively straightforward
- competitors' reactions are predictable
- high-quality data (for example on consumers' tastes) are available

Conducting investment appraisal

There are three techniques of investment appraisal that appear in the AQA specification.

Payback

Payback evaluates individual investment projects in terms of the time taken to recover the original outlay. In the example below, payback in project A is 3 years and project B achieves payback within 2 years.

	Cash flows	
	Project A	**Project B**
Initial investment	(25,000)	(10,000)
Cash inflow year 1	8,000	6,000
Cash inflow year 2	8,000	<u>4,000</u>
Cash inflow year 3	<u>9,000</u>	2,000
Cash inflow year 4	9,000	1,000

Average rate of return

The **average rate of return** assesses the worth of an investment by calculating the yearly percentage return on the sum invested. This calculation uses the formula below:

$$\text{ARR} = \frac{\text{average annual profit}}{\text{initial investment}} \times 100\%$$

The average rate of return allows managers to compare alternative investments, as well as to contrast the percentage rate of return with that available from investing in financial institutions. The table below shows the average rate of return for an investment in an asset expected to last for 6 years.

Total income from investment	Initial cost of investment	Net profit from investment	Average annual profit (over 6 years)	ARR (= average annual profit/ initial cost × 100%)
£220,000	£100,000	£120,000	£20,000	20%

Knowledge check 11

State one weakness of payback and one weakness of ARR as techniques of investment appraisal.

Net present value

NPV uses the technique of discounted cash flow to convert earnings from an investment into their present values — that is, the current worth of money at some time in the future. These present values are then added up and the cost of the investment subtracted from the total. What remains, if anything, is the net present value. NPV must be positive for the investment to be worthwhile. If more than a single investment project is under consideration, the one with the highest NPV will be chosen (if the decision is made on financial grounds). NPV often uses the rate of interest to convert future earnings into current values.

Investment criteria

The results of investment appraisal techniques have to be compared with something in order to make an informed decision. There are two major criteria that a business may use for this purpose.
- **Rate of interest.** Average rate of return and net present value (NPV) methods produce figures that can be compared with the rate of interest. If the average rate of return is used, managers will seek a return that will be greater than the current and forecast interest rates. In the event of using NPV, the interest rate that is current should produce a positive net present value.
- **Other possible investments.** It is unusual for a business to consider only a single investment proposal. Opportunity cost may therefore be an important determinant in which one of several competing investments is selected.

Risks and uncertainties of investment decisions

Risk is the chance of something adverse or bad happening. Investment decisions can go wrong in two main ways: costs may be higher or sales lower than forecast. Forecasting future sales can be a difficult, and often expensive, exercise. Market research can be used, but it is costly and not always reliable. Equally, costs may rise above the forecast level. In many cases, companies are attempting to take decisions about investment projects based on inaccurate data.

Managers may seek to identify and manage the risk in an investment decision by taking a range of actions. These can include purchasing raw materials on forward markets (i.e. setting the price now for future delivery), building in allowances for fluctuations in sales revenue and costs, and ensuring the business has sufficient financial assets available to deal with any adverse circumstances.

Knowledge check 12

Should a business reject an investment opportunity if it is considered to be high risk?

Qualitative influences on investment decisions

A number of qualitative factors are likely to affect investment decisions. These include the following.

- **The business's objectives.** Firms seeking to expand market share may be more willing to invest in projects with a high degree of risk.
- **The image of the business.** Firms such as Virgin, which seeks to appeal to the younger section of the population, are more likely to invest in projects that will enhance this image.
- **Industrial relations.** These are important because major investments frequently have significant implications for the workforce — redundancies, retraining and redeployment are examples.
- **The amount of risk the business is willing to accept.** This will depend upon a number of factors, not least the attitudes of the management team.

Analysis

Themes for analysis could include the following:
- Calculating and interpreting data using investment appraisal techniques.
- Examining the implications of the results of these calculations.
- Examining the advantages and disadvantages of each of the techniques within a specific context.
- Analysing non-financial factors that might affect investment decisions.

Evaluation

- Judging how applicable certain techniques of investment appraisal are in given circumstances.
- Evaluating the relative importance of financial and non-financial factors in reaching decisions regarding investment projects.
- Assessing investment decisions in the context of scenarios and a range of financial and non-financial factors.

Links

Investment decisions relate to many other areas within the specification. These include:
- Human resource planning — for the human implications of investment decisions.
- Marketing — does a demand exist for products that might be produced as a result of the investment?
- The economic environment — how might slump, boom or other economic factors influence the forecast cash flows arising from the investment projects?

Summary

- Objectives are the targets pursued by a business, while the strategy is the medium- to long-term plan to achieve these objectives.

- Corporate objectives and strategies relate to the entire business, whereas functional objectives relate to finance, marketing or other functional areas.

- Businesses pursue a range of financial strategies including cash flow targets, cost minimisation, ROCE targets and shareholders' returns.

- Financial objectives can be influenced by internal and external factors. Examples include the business's corporate objectives and the actions of its rivals.

- Balance sheet and income statements are vital financial documents. Balance sheets record a business's assets and liabilities (and its net worth on a particular day). Working capital and depreciation are important features of balance sheets.

- Income statements record the profit or loss made over a trading period. They include different types of profit and the costs and expenses incurred by the business.

- It is important to compare financial data over time or against those of similar businesses. They may be judged against objectives but beware window dressing.

- Ratio analysis compares two pieces of accounting data and can be used by a range of stakeholders.

- Ratios can be used to assess a business's profitability, financial efficiency, liquidity as well as providing shareholders with important information.

- Ratio analysis allows informed judgements to be made. It has significant limitations, however. It is historical, ignores non-financial issues and may be rendered inaccurate by different accounting policies or the effects of inflation.

- A financial strategy is a medium- to long-term plan designed to achieve the objectives of a business's finance function.

- Financial strategies include raising finance, implementing profit centres, cost minimisation and allocating capital expenditure.

- There are three major techniques of investment appraisal: payback, average rate of return (ARR) and net present value (NPV).

- Payback measures investment decisions in relation to time, while ARR considers profitability. Net present value takes both of these factors into account.

- Investment decisions are frequently subject to uncertainty and therefore risky.

- Investment decisions are subject to a number of qualitative influences, including the business's objectives, its corporate image, relations with the workforce and the amount of risk a business is willing to accept.

Marketing strategies

This section considers the development of marketing strategies for larger businesses through a scientific approach to marketing.

Understanding marketing objectives

Marketing strategy starts with the setting of marketing objectives. **Marketing objectives** are medium- to long-term targets intended to provide a sense of direction for the marketing department. A business might set different marketing objectives, including the following:

- **To increase brand recognition.** This objective may be important for a business that is a new entrant to a market or for most businesses operating in a new market.

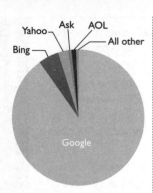

Figure 6 Google's rivals may set marketing objectives to increase their share of the market

Knowledge check 13

What is the difference between market size and market share?

Examiner tip

The type of product sold by a business will determine the impact of economic factors on a business's marketing objectives. For example, if a business sells essential products such as basic foods, changes in the economy may be of limited importance.

- **To increase market share.** This can help to boost revenues and profits. For example, a company might seek to increase its market share from 20% to 25% over 3 years.
- **To broaden its product range in order to improve market standing.** The business may adopt an asset-led approach by using an existing brand name to develop new products.
- **To break into a new market (or market segment).** A business may choose this objective if sales in its existing markets (or segments) are static or falling.

Market share is often illustrated using pie charts in BUSS3 (see Figure 6).

Internal and external influences on marketing objectives

The precise marketing objectives set by a firm will depend upon a variety of factors, the relative importance of which varies from business to business.

Internal factors

- **The business's corporate objectives.** This is clearly a major determinant since the business's marketing objectives should aim to help achieve its corporate objectives. The two sets of objectives should thus be interrelated.
- **The size and type of firm.** Large firms possessing a high degree of market power may set expansive and aggressive marketing objectives. In contrast, new entrants to market or smaller businesses may have objectives that are less ambitious in scope.
- **The financial position of the business.** A business that is profitable or has strong cash flow may be able to engage in the necessary research and development that will enable challenging marketing objectives to be set.
- **The possession of a USP.** A business that has a unique selling point (or proposition) may set objectives reflecting an expectation of substantial increases in market share or brand recognition.

External factors

- **The business's position in the market.** A dominant business may be able to break into new market segments and build upon its existing brand image. Kellogg's provides an example of such an approach.
- **The expected response of competitors.** Whether rivals might match any actions taken to achieve particular marketing objectives can be a major determinant in which objectives are set. This might be particularly the case when the competitors concerned are of similar size and financial power.
- **The state of the economy.** If the economy is growing slowly, or not at all, marketing objectives will be more conservative, especially for businesses that sell luxury items.

Analysis

Themes for analysis could include the following:
- Explaining why a business might choose to adopt a particular marketing objective.
- Examining the possible advantages and disadvantages to a business of adopting a particular marketing objective.
- Considering the major influences on a business's choice of marketing objective.

Evaluation

- Judging the extent to which a business might benefit from pursuing a specific marketing objective in given circumstances.
- Deciding between two (or more) marketing objectives and recommending which might be most suitable in a certain situation.
- Making a judgement on whether internal or external factors were more influential in determining a business's marketing objectives.

Links

There are close links between this and other elements of the Unit 3 marketing specification, particularly marketing strategies and marketing plans.

Marketing objectives also link to other elements of the specification such as innovation — an innovative business is likely to have marketing objectives such as increasing market share and developing new products and product ranges.

Marketing objectives will also link with topics such as workforce plans. A company that sets a marketing objective of entering new markets is likely to have to change its workforce to achieve this target.

Analysing markets and marketing

Reasons for, and the value of, marketing analysis

Businesses take major marketing decisions regularly. It is possible to take two broad approaches to this type of decision making.
- **Decisions based on hunches or instinct.** It is possible for managers to take major marketing decisions, such as whether to introduce a new product, based entirely upon instinct. This means that the management team concerned conducts little or no research and relies upon its knowledge and understanding of the market.
- **Scientific marketing decisions.** Actions of competitors, consumers, suppliers and governments can all have an impact on markets, as can changes in taste and fashion. It is important to gather as much evidence as possible and to consider it carefully before taking major marketing decisions.

Using hunch or instinct might be a valid approach to decision making in a market that regularly experiences rapid change. However, guesswork is risky. For example, incorrectly predicting a surge in demand for a product can result in a business having an embarrassing surplus, with a consequent adverse impact on its cash flow position. The analysis of a market is an expensive exercise, but possibly less so than making a major error in forecasting consumer demand.

Analysis of trends

A **trend** is the underlying pattern of growth or decline within a series of data. Looking at just a few figures may not be helpful, so a firm will attempt to establish any trends. Are sales in a particular area rising, for example? This enables the firm to plan production to meet the demands of the market fully.

Extrapolation analyses the past performance of a variable such as sales and extends this into the future. Establishing the pattern of historic data can help the business to predict what is to happen next. If a firm has enjoyed a steady increase in sales over a number of years, the process of extrapolation is likely to forecast a continued steady rise (see Figure 7).

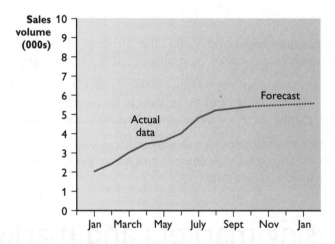

Figure 7 Extrapolation and the trend

Extrapolation:

- is easy to carry out as it merely involves extending a trend
- may be inaccurate as it assumes that the future will be similar to the past
- is not suitable for use in environments subject to rapid change

More scientific approaches to establishing trends may be used. **Moving averages** are a series of calculations designed to show the underlying trend within a series of data. The use of moving averages should smooth out the impact of random variations in data and longer-term cyclical factors, thus highlighting the trend. By predicting trends, firms are able to forecast future sales. **Correlation** is a statistical technique used to establish the extent of the relationship between two variables. It can be an important technique for those involved in marketing as:

- it can show the extent of a relationship (if any) between key variables such as sales and expenditure on promotion

- it can be presented on a graph, as in Figure 8
- it provides information to assist managers in decision making

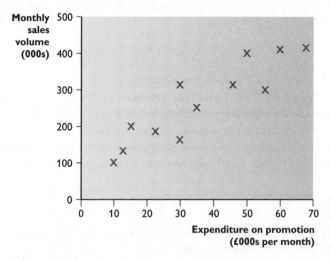

Figure 8 A scatter graph demonstrating close correlation between sales volume and expenditure on promotion

Knowledge check 14

Why do management teams want to establish sales trends for their products?

Ways in which information technology can be used in analysing markets

Collecting marketing data

Information technology is useful to businesses as a means of collecting market research data. This can be done in a variety of ways. For example, consumers' online spending is simple for firms to record and analyse, revealing spending patterns of which managers can take advantage.

A number of supermarkets and other retailers use loyalty cards. One purpose of these cards is to encourage customer loyalty and therefore repeat purchases. However, they also enable the business to collect data on customers' purchases and to relate this to personal data they hold on these customers. In this way, they are able electronically to analyse the types of people who purchase particular products, allowing for better-focused advertising campaigns.

Analysing marketing data

Data that are collected electronically can be analysed in a variety of ways. Using IT, they can also be presented cheaply and quickly in different formats to ensure that all the messages the data contain are understood.

Difficulties in analysing marketing data

Marketing data can give the wrong message for a number of reasons.
- The samples on which the forecasts are based may be too small or unrepresentative.
- Some industries are subject to rapid change. Delays between gathering data and presenting the results to managers may mean that the market has changed.

Examiner tip

An increasing number of businesses operate in global markets, making it more difficult yet more important to collect marketing information. Collecting data is a vital stage in effective marketing.

- Major changes in the external environment can have substantial effects on the decisions of purchasers. A rise in interest rates, for example, may lead to many consumers delaying or abandoning their decision to purchase, especially if a product is to be bought on credit.

Analysis

Themes for analysis could include the following:
- Explaining why a business should (or should not) use market analysis.
- Examining how a particular method of market analysis might help a business to make effective marketing decisions.
- Assessing the reasons why analysing a specific market may be difficult.
- Examining how IT may assist a business in analysing its market.

Evaluation

- Assessing whether a business should invest in a programme of market analysis.
- Judging the value of using IT in market analysis in particular circumstances.
- Considering whether the benefits of market analysis outweigh the drawbacks.

Links

This topic links directly with other elements of the marketing strategies specification. For example, market analysis will help to inform the processes of setting objectives and selecting the 'best' marketing strategy for the circumstances.

It has clear links with operations, in terms of researching and developing new products, as well as setting volume targets.

There are also plenty of links with HR. For instance, when developing and implementing workforce plans, market analysis will inform managers of likely future production types and levels and therefore their workforce needs.

Selecting marketing strategies

Types of marketing strategies

Low cost versus differentiation

A **low-cost marketing strategy** offers a business a way of attracting customers. It can be used by businesses that are late entrants to a market and do not have an established brand name or customer base, and can be highly effective if demand for a product is price elastic. However, it does require the business to have a low cost base and to be able to maintain or reduce its cost levels when established competitors begin to respond to the challenge.

An alternative option is **differentiation**. This means that a business makes its product separate and distinct from those of its rivals, giving consumers a reason to purchase it and to become brand loyal. Differentiation also gives a business the opportunity to charge higher prices, as demand is likely to become more price inelastic.

Ansoff's matrix

A major way to assess a variety of marketing strategies is to use Ansoff's matrix (see Figure 9). Ansoff's **product–market matrix** is illustrated below. It assists businesses in evaluating themselves and the markets in which they operate by considering the relationship between marketing and overall corporate strategy.

The matrix considers product and market growth and analyses the degree of risk attached to the range of options open to the business. The key findings of Ansoff's matrix include the following:

- Staying with what you know (e.g. market penetration) represents relatively little risk.
- Moving into new markets with new products is a high-risk strategy.
- Assessment is made of the value of each option.

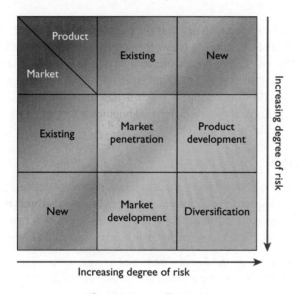

Figure 9 Ansoff's matrix

Examiner tip

Ansoff's matrix is a valuable tool for explaining marketing decisions and for justifying them in terms of risk. For example, you might use it to explain and justify why a firm selling low-cost products might pursue a strategy of market penetration.

Market penetration

A strategy of market penetration means that a business has chosen to market existing products to its existing customers more strongly. By making this choice, the business avoids the expense and time involved in developing new products or investigating and analysing unfamiliar markets. As a result, the strategy can be implemented relatively quickly and cheaply.

However, it may be that the market is saturated (few, if any, new customers exist) and therefore the only way to increase sales is by taking customers away from competitors. A policy of market penetration can necessitate heavy expenditure on promotion and some flexibility in pricing decisions. Because this marketing strategy does not involve new products or new markets, it is categorised as low risk.

Knowledge check 15

What marketing strategies might a business adopt when operating in a saturated market?

Market development

This strategy involves a business targeting its existing product range at potential customers in a new market. This means that the product remains the same, but it is marketed to a new audience. New markets could be overseas or possibly a different segment within a domestic market.

This strategy is classified as medium risk because the product or products are unchanged and the business's managers are presumably familiar with their strengths and weaknesses. It also avoids the need for developing new products, which can be costly and time-consuming. However, the products may not be accepted in the new markets or they may need expensive modifications.

Product development

This strategy means that a new product is marketed to a business's existing customers. The business develops and innovates new product offerings to replace or supplement existing ones.

The advantages of this approach are that the business knows its customers and is in contact with them already, making it easier to conduct market research and promote new products. The business may also have a strong brand name that it can attach to its new products. The downside of this strategy is that the business may engage in producing and selling products in which it has limited expertise and it may be vulnerable to the actions of more established businesses in the market. This strategy is categorised by Ansoff as medium risk.

Diversification

This is where a business's marketing strategy is to sell completely new products to new customers. There are two types of diversification. **Related diversification** means that a business remains in a market or industry with which it is familiar. **Unrelated diversification** is where it has no previous industry or market experience.

This is a high-risk strategy, as the business lacks experience of the product and the customer base that it is targeting. As a consequence, it will have greater need of market analysis to guide its marketing decisions.

How to assess the effectiveness of marketing strategies

The best way to assess the effectiveness of a particular marketing strategy is to compare it to the marketing objectives that were set prior to its implementation. If these objectives have been fulfilled, the strategy can be deemed to have been successful. Another key means of judgement is to assess the extent to which the marketing strategy has enabled the business to achieve its corporate objectives.

Other measures can be applied as well. It may be that a successful marketing strategy will result in other businesses copying it.

Knowledge check 16

What difficulties might a business encounter when entering a new market overseas?

Knowledge check 17

Why might a business decide on a high-risk strategy such as diversification?

Analysis

Themes for analysis could include the following:

- Examining the risks and benefits of particular marketing strategies.
- Explaining why some marketing strategies are riskier than others.

Evaluation

- Assessing whether a business should adopt a given marketing strategy.
- Making a judgement about the best marketing strategy in particular circumstances.
- Assessing the value of a particular marketing strategy when entering a given market, including international markets.

Links

This topic links directly with other elements of the marketing strategies specification. For example, marketing objectives and marketing strategies should be interrelated. A marketing strategy will also be set out in the business's marketing plan.

Marketing strategy also links with operations in terms of location (the business may produce in the new markets in which it intends to sell) and innovation (when there is a strategy of product development).

The business's financial position is likely to determine its marketing strategy to some degree. For example, cash flow difficulties might limit strategies of market and product development.

Developing and implementing marketing plans

Marketing planning involves developing the tactics necessary to implement the marketing strategy, for example:

- establishing targets for marketing
- coordinating the different elements of the mix
- deciding on an overall budget for marketing
- setting deadlines — deciding by when marketing objectives should be achieved

A **marketing plan** is a document setting out the strategy a business will use to achieve its marketing objectives. The plan will include the following:

- marketing targets that the firm is attempting to achieve
- the elements of the marketing mix to be used and how they will be coordinated
- the timescale to which the plan relates
- the resources available to fund the marketing plan. This section will include a marketing budget

A marketing plan for a large organisation might bring together a number of separate marketing plans for individual goods and services.

> **Examiner tip**
> Do make sure you know exactly what a marketing plan is and what it contains. Many answers on marketing plans tend to be vague in this way, which can limit the marks that the examiner awards.

Key components of a marketing plan

Marketing objectives

The plan will detail the marketing objectives that the business intends to achieve, along with anticipated timescales.

Marketing budgets

A marketing budget is the amount of money that a business allocates for expenditure on marketing activities over a particular period of time. These activities will include advertising, sales promotions, public relations and market research.

The size of a firm's marketing budget will be determined by a number of factors.
- **The financial position of the business.** If a business is recording rising profits, it is likely to be able to fund higher levels of expenditure on advertising and other marketing activities.
- **The actions of competitors.** If a business's rivals are increasing expenditure on marketing activities, it is likely that the firm in question will follow suit.
- **The business's marketing objectives.** If a firm has set objectives such as increasing market share or extending its product range, it is likely to spend heavily on marketing.

Sales forecasts

Examiner tip
Do look in the BUSS3 case study for evidence on how sales forecasts were compiled to judge their likely accuracy. Important evidence may include: is the business experienced in this market, how volatile is the market and how much primary market research was conducted?

Good forecasting is a key component of business success. Forecasts are usually made for a number of different elements:
- sales of product(s)
- costs for the forthcoming accounting period
- cash flow
- key economic variables such as inflation, unemployment, exchange rates and incomes

Time-series analysis involves making forecasts from past figures. A firm is able to predict future sales by analysing its sales figures over previous years.

Major internal and external influences on marketing plans

There are a number of main influences on any company's marketing plan.
- **Finance available to the business.** This is an obvious influence on the marketing budget, but it can also influence the approach to sales forecasting (i.e. how extensive it is, as well as the timescale and the specific marketing mix that is to be used). Access to larger funds allows a business to set more challenging marketing objectives and more extensive promotional campaigns and programmes of new product development.
- **Operational issues.** A business can only put in its marketing plan what it can actually deliver. Thus, the available operational resources will act as a constraint. For example, the business's productive capacity may determine the number of markets in which it can operate.
- **Competitors' actions.** For businesses trading in markets that are dominated by a few large firms, it is common to consider the likely reactions of competitors

as an integral part of planning. Sales forecasts will be drawn up carefully and underpinned with assumptions about what rivals might do.

Issues in implementing marketing plans

Marketing planning may be important for a business that has recently started trading or for one considering a major change, such as entering a new market. However, marketing plans do not always work quite as intended.

Knowledge check 18

Why might a marketing plan not always work as expected?

Benefits of marketing planning

Businesses can gain significant benefits from drawing up marketing plans.
- Plans help to give a sense of direction to all employees within the business.
- Managers can compare their achievement with the plan and take the necessary action if they are not on target.
- Planning is a good process in itself. It encourages managers to think ahead and to weigh up the options available, as well as threats and opportunities.
- Effective marketing plans establish targets that are realistic and achievable, that motivate the staff involved and that can be afforded by the business concerned.

Potential problems in marketing planning

But plans have to be treated with caution too.
- Drawing up a marketing plan takes time and resources. In a rapidly changing marketplace, this might not be the optimal approach, as quick decisions (possibly based on hunches) might be required.
- Plans might cause managers to be inflexible and not to respond to changes in the marketplace. Sometimes it might be more important to change the marketing targets than to achieve them.

Analysis

Opportunities for analysis include:
- Arguing the benefits of this type of planning to a particular firm or in a given scenario.
- Explaining factors that may cause firms not to plan their marketing.
- Examining the implications for a firm of a decision to engage in marketing planning.
- Explaining why the results of sales forecasting might be inaccurate (or accurate) and the actions businesses might take to improve accuracy.
- Examining the key influences on a business's marketing plan.

Evaluation

- Assessing the overall benefits of planning, as the adoption of detailed marketing planning may entail additional short-term costs with benefits only being realised in the long term.
- Evaluating whether this approach to marketing, with its emphasis on internal communication and consultation, fits with the leadership style, corporate culture etc.

- Considering the speed of change in the market — rapid change may invalidate marketing planning.
- Realising that the size of the marketing budget is not all-important — success will also depend upon the skill of the marketing team (and others) and actions of competitors.
- Considering the factors which are likely to enable a given firm to achieve accurate sales forecasts.

Links

This topic links with many others.

- Within marketing, issues such as price elasticity of demand, product portfolio analysis and market research may all be relevant topics.
- Important links also exist with finance: liquidity and profitability will influence marketing budgets; sales forecasts will affect cash flow and forecast revenues.
- Marketing planning (especially sales forecasting) has significant implications for production in terms of range and scale of output.
- HR planning will be affected by sales forecasts, as expected sales figures are a vital determinant of the number and types of employees required.

Summary

- Marketing objectives are medium- to long-term plans intended to provide a sense of direction to a business.
- Businesses pursue a range of marketing objectives, including increasing brand recognition and market share or extending a product range.
- Internal and external factors, such as the size and type of firm and the expected response of competitors, can influence marketing objectives.
- Businesses can take marketing decisions on the basis of hunch or as a result of a scientific approach to decision making.
- Trends in marketing data can be forecast using extrapolation, moving averages or correlation. Identifying future trends assists a business in forecasting sales.
- Technology can be used to gather marketing data. Supermarkets use loyalty cards to collect data on their consumers.
- IT can also be used to analyse marketing data. However, it may be difficult to analyse these data as samples may be too small or the external environment may change.
- A marketing strategy is a medium- to long-term plan to achieve a business's marketing objectives. Examples include low cost and differentiation.

- Ansoff's matrix can be used to assess marketing strategies in terms of risk by classifying them into four groups: market penetration, product development, market development and diversification.
- The success of a marketing strategy can be judged by the extent to which it enables a business to achieve its marketing objectives.
- A marketing plan sets out the strategy a business will use to achieve its marketing objectives. Marketing planning develops the tactics to implement the marketing strategy.
- The main components of a marketing plan include the marketing objectives, marketing budgets and sales forecasts.
- The internal influences on a marketing plan may include the finance available and operational issues. Actions of competitors are an external influence.
- The benefits of marketing plans are that they can provide a sense of direction to employees, encouraging managers to monitor progress of marketing decisions and to think ahead.
- Marketing plans require significant amounts of precious resources and may lead to managers becoming inflexible and refusing to move away from the plan, even when this may be beneficial.

Operational strategies

This section considers the operational objectives and strategies that a business may use to achieve success in a particular market.

Understanding operational objectives

Nature of operational objectives

Operational objectives are the targets pursued by the operations function or department of a business. There are a number of operational objectives, the importance of which will vary according to the type of business, its products and market.

Quality targets

A quality product is one that meets customers' needs fully. A business may set itself a number of quality targets.

- A specific percentage of faulty products. This type of target can be used in manufacturing and service contexts. For an insurance company, it could relate to the number of errors in documentation, while in a manufacturing context it could be goods that do not operate properly.
- The implementation of quality standards, usually within a specific timescale. Many businesses adopt quality standards, most notably ISO 9000. This is intended to assure customers that the business has appropriate procedures for ensuring the supply of quality products.

Cost and volume targets

- **Cost targets.** A business may set itself a unit cost target — that is, it will aim to produce its products at or below a stated average or unit cost.
- **Volume targets.** These exist when a business plans to produce more than a certain amount of output. Having such targets may help to increase market share and raise the profile of a business or brand, but does not guarantee specific profit levels.

Innovation

Innovation is the creation of new ideas and the successful development of products from these ideas. Innovation can also relate to new ways of making products. A business may set itself a target of being innovative and of bringing a certain number of new products to the market each year. Innovation is more likely to be an operational target for businesses operating in fashion and technological markets.

Knowledge check 19

What is the difference between invention and innovation?

Efficiency

An efficient business produces the maximum number of outputs (goods and services) with the minimum number of inputs (labour, capital, raw materials, fuel, time etc.). Efficiency can take a number of forms.

- **Cost efficiency.** Cost-efficient firms produce products very cheaply, which may be highly attractive to certain groups of customers.
- **Resource efficiency.** Businesses aim to produce very little waste as a consequence of their production processes. This may involve the recycling of off-cuts and of any heat or water produced as a by-product.
- **Time efficiency.** Another way of considering the efficiency of a business is to measure time. For example, Japanese car manufacturers have a record of developing new products more quickly than many of their competitors.

Environmental targets

For many organisations, this type of operational target is assuming ever-greater importance. For industries in the so-called 'polluting sector' (oil and chemical businesses, for example), setting and meeting environmental targets is a vital aspect of management. Environmental targets include:

- reducing or eliminating the use of non-sustainable resources
- reducing carbon emissions and the business's 'carbon footprint'
- cutting back on the amount of waste produced in the production process
- achieving targets for recycling — often expressed in terms of percentages

Internal and external influences on operational objectives

Internal influences on operational objectives may include the following:

- **Corporate objectives of the business.** The corporate and operations objectives of the business should be consistent and should not conflict. So a business with a corporate objective of growth, for example, may choose cost targets as prime operational objectives to allow it to reduce prices in the expectation of increasing sales and market share.

- **Financial position of the business.** A business may be unable to afford to invest in machinery to meet self-imposed environmental targets if it has endured a poor trading period.
- **Nature of the product.** For manufacturing firms, environmental issues and targets may be given a higher priority. A business selling a luxury product is more likely to set targets in terms of quality, while time-based targets may be given prominence in the fashion industry.

External influences on operational objectives can take a number of forms:

- **Operational objectives of competitors.** It may be that consumers compare the products supplied by different firms. In this case, businesses may need to match the operational objectives of their rivals.
- **Legislation.** The UK government and EU authorities have imposed laws that impact the operational objectives that firms can set themselves (e.g. most businesses supplying services are subject to safety laws designed to protect consumers).

- **Tastes and fashions.** If a business expects regular changes in the tastes and fashions of its customers, it may set itself time-based operational targets in order to meet their needs as soon as possible.

Analysis

Opportunities for analysis include:
- Arguing the benefits of setting operational benefits of any type, or of setting specific operational targets.
- Explaining why particular businesses benefit from setting specific operational targets.
- Examining the major influences on the operational targets set by a particular business.

Evaluation

- Assessing the case for and against the setting of operational targets in specific circumstances.
- Judging the major influence on the operational objectives set by a business.

Links

The following links exist from this topic:
- Within the remainder of operations, the precise objectives set will influence the scale and resource mix used (see page 45) and whether the business adopts lean production techniques. Emphasis on cost targets may influence location, as some businesses have moved to Eastern Europe and China to reduce production costs.
- Targets in terms of innovation will influence both the marketing strategies and marketing objectives that a business adopts.
- Cost and volume targets are closely linked with finance and have implications for costs, revenues, profits and cash flow.
- Innovation and environmental targets may lead to increased demand for certain types of employees and thereby have implications for recruitment, training and workforce planning.

Operational strategies: scale and resource mix

Economies and diseconomies of scale

As firms grow in size, they begin to benefit from **economies of scale**. This means that unit production costs fall and, up to a point, efficiency and profits improve (see Figure 10 on page 44). This allows businesses to reduce the cost of producing a unit of output and gives them the chance to sell at lower prices while maintaining profit margins.

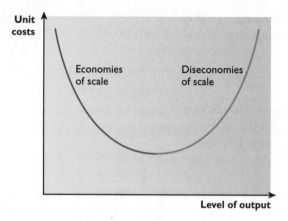

Figure 10 Many businesses face U-shaped unit cost curves

Internal economies of scale

Internal economies of scale are those factors that reduce unit or average costs in an individual firm as it increases the scale of its operations. Examples include:

- **Purchasing economies**, which exist when firms are able to buy components and materials more cheaply, taking advantage of bulk discounts.
- **Production economies**, which arise from the use of mass production techniques to speed up production. Firms producing greater quantities can afford to buy large, specialised, technically advanced machinery to lower production costs.
- **Financial economies**, which offer significant advantages to larger enterprises. Such firms are able to borrow more easily and at more favourable rates of interest, as they have greater reserves.
- **Marketing economies**, which reduce unit costs because firms can afford to advertise extensively — the extra cost is small when spread over many units of output.

External economies of scale

External economies of scale are the advantages of scale that benefit a whole industry, not just individual firms. So if an industry is concentrated in one geographical area, the following benefits might be available to all the firms:

- a network of suppliers
- skilled labour
- training courses at local colleges
- a suitable infrastructure — roads, rail links etc.

Note that external economies of scale are based on the size and concentration of the industry, rather than the firm.

Diseconomies of scale

Large firms can also suffer from diseconomies of scale. Once they are past their minimum efficient scale, the cost per unit of production begins to increase (see Figure 10). This may be due to:

- **Over-use of existing machinery.** This increases maintenance costs and causes breakdowns.

Knowledge check 20

What effect would you expect the existence of economies of scale to have on a business's profit margins as it increases its level of output?

- **Communication problems.** As the business grows, people may not know who to report to. Managers may begin to rely on sending e-mails rather than speaking to people directly.
- **Marketing problems.** Managers may not concentrate on the right products.

The fact that large businesses are not necessarily more profitable than small or medium-sized businesses is evidence that diseconomies of scale do operate in the real world.

Capital and labour intensity

Capital-intensive production occurs when the production of the good or service relies more heavily on capital (equipment and machinery, for example) than on other factors of production. Labour-intensive production relies more heavily on the use of labour.

Choosing the resource mix

Deciding on the right mix of labour and capital depends on a number of factors.

- **Size of the business.** It may be that a larger firm is able to justify (and afford) using types of technology in its production that a smaller business could not.
- **Type of product.** If a business produces large quantities of standard products, it may be feasible to use a greater proportion of capital in the production process. This would not be sensible for a business that produces more individual products made to the order of specific customers.
- **Finance available to the business.** Adopting capital-intensive production systems can be an expensive option. Not only does the business have to invest in the capital equipment, but it may also face substantial expenditure in training its employees to use the equipment efficiently.

Advantages and disadvantages

Labour-intensive production can lead to increased costs of recruitment, selection and training. It is also possible that labour disputes can lead to serious disruption of production. On the plus side, labour-intensive production may allow the business to claim a unique selling point.

Capital-intensive production may help businesses to reduce their unit costs of production and to produce standard goods that meet agreed specifications, including quality targets. Capital-intensive businesses may also be able to be more flexible in terms of quantity of output. However, the major drawback is cost.

Analysis

Opportunities for analysis include:

- Examining the financial and other benefits to a business of changing the scale of its production.
- Explaining the benefits and drawbacks of labour- and capital-intensive production.
- Arguing the case for a business adopting labour-intensive (or capital-intensive) production.

Evaluation

- Assessing the case for a business moving to capital- or labour-intensive production.
- Judging whether a business should increase (or decrease) its scale of production.

Links

The following links exist from this topic:

- The scale and resource mix used by a business may help it to achieve its operational objectives. The resource mix links closely with location, as a move to places with lower labour costs may result in increased labour intensity.
- Economies and diseconomies of scale have links with marketing, as they may allow (or make difficult) more competitive pricing and a strategy of market penetration.
- This topic also links with financial strategies (cost minimisation, for example) and can affect financial performance through profit margins.

Operational strategies: innovation

Research and development (R&D) is the creation of new ideas and the successful development of products from these ideas. Innovation is the scientific investigation leading to new ideas for products *and* the development of those ideas into saleable products.

Purpose, costs, benefits and risk of innovation

Purpose of innovation

Innovation takes place before a product is launched — that is, before the product life cycle starts. This may result in the business facing difficulties with its cash flow, but it may be able to subsidise new products from more established ones. Once products enter the growth and maturity stages of their life cycle, it might be appropriate for the business to invest in innovation for the next generation of products. This may need to occur even earlier if the new products are likely to take time to develop. The purpose of innovation is to give a business a competitive edge. Bringing new products onto the market before rivals do allows a company to charge premium prices, thereby boosting profits.

Benefits of innovation

- Businesses can gain a significant competitive advantage by being the first to bring a new product on to the market. An innovative product with no direct rivals allows firms to charge high prices.
- Businesses can gain a reputation for producing high-quality and sophisticated products. Acquiring a reputation for supplying innovative products can boost sales of other, related products and increase profit margins, as shown in Figure 11.

- Patents can be used to protect business ideas for a period of up to 20 years, allowing inventors to generate substantial earnings from their research and innovation. Many companies allow other businesses to produce their ideas under licence.

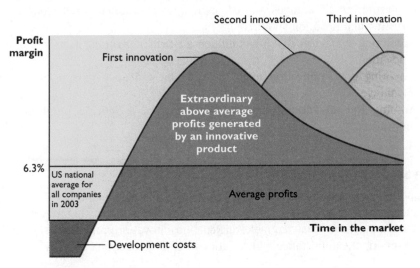

Figure 11 Successful innovation can boost profit margins

Disadvantages of innovation

- Research can be very expensive and only large firms can afford to engage in it.
- The timescale can be lengthy, meaning investors have to wait a long time for a return on their money. This may not be viable unless a business has other profitable products on the market at the same time.
- Other companies may adopt 'me too' products that are similar (but not too similar) to a new product, without having to undertake the expensive research. This can lead to a loss of sales and profits.
- To succeed in highly competitive markets, firms must continuously innovate and sell new products. This requires continuous investment.

Innovation and risk

There are a number of reasons why a strategy of innovation can be risky.

- **The innovative product may fail.** Only a small number of products that are developed actually succeed. This means that firms spend enormous sums of money on projects that do not generate any returns.
- **Other firms may copy an innovative product.** This can be a major problem for a business that has incurred all the research and development costs without the benefits of selling large numbers of premium-priced products.

Businesses can protect their ideas in a number of ways.

- Patents provide protection for products and processes for a period of up to 20 years.
- Copyrights provide protection for the creators and owners of books, music and cartoons. They can last for up to 70 years after the death of the author and are granted automatically.
- Trademarks grant legal ownership of recognisable signs and symbols for an indefinite period.

Examiner tip
Remember that innovation is an appropriate strategy in some industries, such as electronic products and motor vehicle manufacture. If the BUSS3 case study covers such businesses, this may be a relevant strategy to propose.

Knowledge check 22
How might a business respond to the emergence of copycat or 'me-too' products?

Analysis

Opportunities for analysis exist in the following areas:

- Analysing the advantages and disadvantages that might result from a firm investing in innovation and R&D.
- Examining the factors that might influence a firm in planning its programme of innovation.
- Exploring how innovation might be used by a firm to gain a competitive advantage.
- Arguing the advantages and disadvantages of a specific programme of innovation.

Evaluation

Opportunities exist for evaluation in a number of areas, including:

- Judging the case for and against a business investing heavily in innovation.
- Evaluating factors that may make an R&D and innovation programme successful.
- Assessing the importance of innovation to an organisation's success.

Links

Innovation links to finance in a variety of ways — investment decision making is one example.

Innovation also has close links with marketing, including topics such as marketing objectives and marketing strategies, especially product development.

There are many links between innovation and various topics within operational strategies, notably capital intensity and lean production.

Operational strategies: location

The location of a business depends upon a variety of factors:

- the proximity of natural resources, components and other supplies
- the local infrastructure
- the whereabouts of the market in which the business sells its products
- government actions, for example grants and other forms of financial support
- qualitative factors such as the quality of life that senior employees might expect from working and living in that place

Profit-making businesses seek to identify the least-cost location. It is quite usual for firms to use financial techniques to assess the suitability of one or more locations.

- Break-even analysis can be used to calculate costs and revenues of possible locations and the level of sales required for profitability.
- Investment appraisal techniques can be used to select the location offering the greatest return over some specified period of time.

Knowledge check 23

What factors might influence the location of a retailer that sells its products using the internet?

Multi-site location

It is not unusual for large businesses to operate on more than one site. This can be in a single country or in many countries. Multi-site location creates a number of advantages and disadvantages, as set out below. The major advantages are:

- A multi-site location permits a business to be closer to its markets and to monitor market trends better.
- Multi-site locations can give a business a prestigious address as well as the benefits of cheaper sites elsewhere.
- Some large businesses are in effect several smaller businesses operating as a conglomerate. Having a number of locations allows each element of the business to be in its optimal place.
- It becomes possible for firms to operate on a large scale without all the potential problems of diseconomies of scale.

The disadvantages include the following:

- Communication is more problematic, as employees may be unable to meet face to face.
- The business may incur greater operating costs if materials need to be transported between the various sites.
- It may be necessary to relocate employees from one site to another, which could meet with resistance from those who are settled with family ties in a particular location.

Knowledge check 24

Why might multi-site locations encourage greater decentralisation?

International location

Firms taking decisions on international locations will consider a number of important factors:

- effective communications and transport networks
- trained and productive labour available at competitive rates of pay
- low rates of taxation levied on business profits
- grants and support available from local and national governments to support the heavy investment necessary
- whether support services (for example component suppliers) are readily available

They may also take into account a number of broader issues:

- Is the country in which they are considering locating politically stable?
- Is the company likely to suffer from exchange rate fluctuations as a consequence of its decision?
- Will the company avoid tariffs or other trade barriers by locating in a particular country?

Examiner tip

Many BUSS3 papers consider international location, so it is important to ensure that your study of this topic takes global dimension.

Analysis

Opportunities for analysis exist in a number of areas:

- Arguing the case for locating in a particular site.
- Explaining the benefits of locating in an optimal location.
- Examining the advantages and disadvantages of choosing to operate on more than a single site.

Evaluation

There are also several opportunities for evaluation within this area of the specification:

- Weighing up the case for a business opting for a multi-site location.
- Assessing the 'best' location for a firm in a particular scenario.
- Evaluating the most important factor(s) in a business's location decisions.

Links

Location has links with virtually every other area of the specification. A location decision impacts on finance, marketing and human resources, as well as having implications for many other topics within operations such as scale and resource mix.

Operational strategies: lean production

The concept of lean production is increasingly used to describe the organisational goals of manufacturing industry. This term describes a range of measures designed to use fewer inputs and resources. The measures include:

- just-in-time production
- kaizen or continuous improvement
- time-based management and simultaneous engineering

How businesses manage time effectively

Time-based management

Time-based management seeks to shorten all aspects of production to reduce costs and make it easier to meet the needs of consumers.

Lean producers are characterised by short product development times. Toyota, for example, habitually develops products from the drawing board to the marketplace more quickly than its rivals.

Having short product development times offers a number of benefits:

- It may prove less costly, as less time and fewer resources are devoted to research and development.
- A firm that is first to launch a product on to the market can charge a higher price and enjoy higher profits.
- Being the market leader in this way can motivate the workforce.

Simultaneous engineering

Simultaneous engineering manages the development of new products in the shortest possible time. Some aspects of production development can be carried out at the

Knowledge check 25

What disadvantages might result from developing products quickly and being first on the market?

same time, enabling products to get on to the market faster, cutting costs and generating revenue earlier than would otherwise have been the case.

Critical path analysis

Critical path analysis (CPA) is one type of network analysis. It is a method of calculating and illustrating how complex projects can be completed as quickly as possible. CPA shows:

- the sequence in which the tasks must be undertaken
- the length of time taken by each task
- the earliest time at which each stage can commence

A CPA network consists of two elements:

- **Activities.** This is part of a project requiring time and the firm's resources. The lines (running from left to right) show the sequence of the tasks.
- **Nodes.** These are the start or finish of an activity and are represented by circles. Each node is numbered (in the left-hand segment) and also states the 'earliest start time' (EST) and 'latest finish time' (LFT) (see Figure 12).

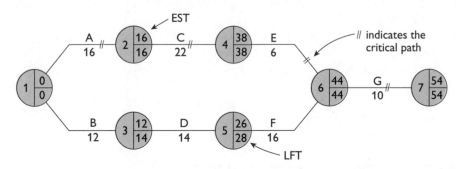

Figure 12 A critical path network

The earliest start times (EST) show the earliest times at which particular activities can be commenced. The EST on the final node shows the earliest date at which the whole project can be concluded. The latest finish time (LFT) records the time by which an activity must be completed, if the entire project is not to be delayed.

CPA offers businesses several advantages:

- It involves managers in detailed planning, which helps to reduce the risk of delays and other problems.
- Resources needed for each activity may be made available at the appropriate time, thus reducing costs — in particular the need for working capital.
- Time can be saved by operating certain activities simultaneously, possibly creating competitive advantage.
- The information from CPA assists managers in making high-quality decisions.

But as with many techniques in business, there are disadvantages too:

- Complex activities may be impossible to represent accurately on a network.
- The project still requires management even after the initial network is drawn up, as external factors may change.
- CPA relies on estimates for the expected duration of activities — if these are inaccurate the whole process may be invalidated.

Examiner tip
You will not be asked to draw a CPA network as part of your BUSS3 examination. You may, however, have to complete one by, for example, calculating ESTs and LFTs.

Examiner tip
Do not simply focus on the CPA network in your revision. Many questions ask about the issues and benefits involved in their use.

Other elements of lean production

Just-in-time manufacturing

Just-in-time (JIT) manufacturing is a Japanese management philosophy that involves having the right items of the right quality in the right place at the right time. JIT is a central component of lean production.

Just-in-time manufacturing is not one technique or even a set of techniques, but an overall philosophy embracing both old and new techniques. The philosophy is based on eliminating waste. Thus JIT means using the minimum amount of resources to satisfy customer demand.

The key characteristics of JIT are:
- It allows an organisation to meet consumer demand at whatever level it exists. JIT is a 'pull' system of production.
- It is based on demand–pull production — demand signals when a product should be manufactured.
- Suppliers of components and other materials must be very responsive to orders from the manufacturer.
- It allows a reduction in raw materials, work-in-progress and finished goods inventories. This frees up a greater amount of space within factories.
- It requires high levels of training to give workers the skills necessary to carry out a number of tasks.
- Employees engage in self-inspection to ensure that their products are of high quality and that value has been added.
- Continuous improvement is an integral part of JIT.

Kaizen or continuous improvement

Kaizen means 'continuous improvement' and is a very important element of lean production. It entails continual but small advances in production techniques, each improving productivity a little.
- Kaizen groups meet regularly to discuss problems and to propose new ideas to improve productivity.
- The improvements proposed under the kaizen system cost relatively little but can have a substantial impact on costs of production.
- Lean production invites shop-floor ideas to produce regular and small-scale improvements in productivity, which are less likely to create job losses and damage morale.

The implementation of a kaizen policy has implications for a business's workforce:
- All employees should be continually seeking ways to improve their performance through new approaches and techniques.
- Team working is an integral element of continuous improvement. Teams can be the basis of kaizen groups designed to provide ideas and solve problems.
- Empowerment gives employees control over their working lives. Empowered employees will feel confident in proposing ideas and have the authority to implement their decisions.

- Training is an important component of kaizen. Employees need new skills if they are to fulfil a number of roles within the team.

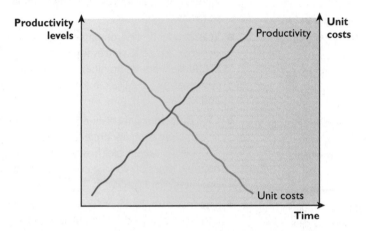

Figure 13 The effects of a successful policy of kaizen can increase the productivity of a business's workforce and result in a reduction in unit costs of production. This may allow the business to increase competitiveness by lowering prices or to receive a higher profit margin

Analysis

Opportunities for analysis exist in the following areas:
- Completing and interpreting a CPA network.
- Analysing the implications for businesses of the use of CPA.
- Highlighting the benefits and drawbacks of CPA or elements of lean production.
- Arguing the benefits that a firm might gain from the use of one or more elements of lean production.
- Highlighting the drawbacks that may arise from the use of CPA.

Evaluation

A number of evaluative themes may be explored, including the following:
- Assessing the impact of CPA on the competitive performance of a business.
- Judging the consequences of a change in the duration of an activity on the critical path of a network.
- Evaluating the value of CPA or lean production techniques in specific circumstances.

Links

The techniques of lean production and CPA relate closely to diverse areas of the specification, including the management of cash flow, training (to provide employees with necessary new skills), the development of new products, financial strategies such as cost minimisation and investment decisions.

Summary

- Operational objectives are the targets pursued by the operations department of a business.

- Quality is an important operational target and may encompass minimising faults and implementing quality standards.

- Other operational targets include innovation, increasing efficiency and protecting the environment.

- Internal influences on operational objectives include the business's financial position and corporate objectives. Tastes and fashions and competitors' actions are external influences on objectives.

- Economies of scale benefit businesses by reducing unit costs as output rises, allowing price reductions without reducing profit margins. Diseconomies of scale have the opposite effect as firms become very large.

- Firms choose a mix of resources to use in production and may opt to be labour intensive or to rely on capital (capital intensive).

- Innovation is the development of new ideas and their conversion into successful products and processes. Innovation can bring significant competitive advantages.

- Innovation is an expensive option and risky as new products may fail.

- The location of a business depends on a variety of factors, including availability of supplies, transport links and the proximity to markets.

- Most businesses seek the lowest-cost location and increasingly this involves multi-site locations, often in a number of countries.

- Lean production encompasses a range of measures designed to use fewer resources. Techniques of lean production include simultaneous engineering, critical path analysis (CPA), just-in-time (JIT) manufacturing and kaizen.

- CPA is a planning technique that allows businesses to complete complex projects as quickly as possible. Its use enables businesses to operate with reduced levels of working capital and to launch new products more quickly.

- The major weakness of CPA is its reliance on estimates of time durations of activities, which are notoriously difficult to forecast.

- JIT manufacturing is a philosophy based on eliminating waste and uses minimal resources to satisfy demand. It involves 'pull' systems of production, fewer resources and skilled employees.

- Kaizen means 'continuous improvement'. Its successful use can improve productivity levels and a business's competitiveness. It does require expenditure on training to equip employees with new skills but can have positive effects on motivation.

Human resource strategies

Understanding HR objectives and strategies

Human resource objectives are the targets pursued by the HR function or department of the business. The achievement of these goals should assist the business in attaining its corporate objectives. The main HR objectives are as discussed below.

Knowledge check 27

How might a business improve the skills of its workforce?

Matching the workforce's skills to the needs of the business

As a business grows, moves overseas, introduces different products or uses more technology in production, it will require a different workforce. The HR department will need to recruit new employees, make some redundant and redeploy others, as well as training them to provide the necessary skills.

Making full use of the workforce's potential

A workforce's potential may be underused because:

- **Skills are untapped.** It is possible that employees have some skills which they do not use as part of their working lives.
- **Employees are underutilised.** Some may find that their jobs are not challenging — they may not stretch them or use their talents to their full extent.

HR departments may have an objective to overcome such difficulties.

Knowledge check 28

Why might a business want to make full use of its workforce's potential?

Maintaining good employer–employee relations

Maintaining good relations with employees is an important HR objective for most businesses because:

- it makes expensive strikes and other forms of labour dispute less likely
- research has shown that businesses with good industrial relations attract higher-calibre applicants
- good employer–employee relations assist a business to maintain a positive corporate image, which may boost sales

Knowledge check 29

What is meant by good employer–employee relations?

Internal and external influences on HR objectives

Internal influences on HR objectives

- **Corporate objectives.** Objectives set by the HR department must assist the organisation in achieving its overall objectives.
- **Attitudes and beliefs of senior managers.** If senior managers consider the workforce to be a valuable asset, they are likely to want the relationship with employees to be long term and may set objectives such as developing the skills of the workforce to their fullest extent. Alternatively they may see employees as an expendable asset, to be hired when necessary and paid the minimum rate possible.
- **Type of product.** If a product requires the commitment of a highly skilled labour force, then objectives such as making the full use of the workforce's potential may be most important. However, for businesses selling products which are mainly produced by machinery and require little skilled labour, then minimising labour costs may be a key HR objective.

External influences on HR objectives

- **Price elasticity of demand for the product.** When demand for a product is strongly price elastic, it is more likely that a business will opt for HR objectives that allow it to reduce labour costs.
- **Corporate image.** Most businesses will set HR objectives that include maintaining good relations with employees to avoid damaging the company's image.
- **Employment legislation.** UK and EU laws may make it difficult to hire and fire employees, thereby encouraging businesses to set HR objectives to develop workforce potential.

Knowledge check 30

Why might having good employer–employee relations improve a business's corporate image?

HR strategies

Not all businesses take the same view of HR strategies, and two broad approaches have emerged:

- **'Hard' HR strategies.** The 'hard' approach to HR strategy views employees as a resource to be used as efficiently as possible. In this way, they are no different from vehicles or production machinery. Employees are hired as cheaply as possible, managed closely and made redundant when no longer required.
- **'Soft' HR strategies.** The 'soft' approach is based on the belief that employees are perhaps the most valuable asset a business possesses. Thus it is in the company's interest to maximise their value, developing them over time to help make the business competitive in the marketplace.

Analysis

Opportunities for analysis exist in the following areas:
- Explaining why a specific business may adopt certain HR objectives.
- Examining the main external and internal influences on the HR objectives selected by a business.
- Analysing the strengths and weaknesses of 'hard' and 'soft' HR strategies.

Evaluation

A number of evaluative themes may be explored, including the following:
- Arguing the case for and against using a particular HR strategy.
- Judging the most important influence on a business's HR objectives.
- Assessing why a business might adopt a 'hard' or a 'soft' HR strategy.

Links

This topic links with various financial strategies. For example, implementing profit centres may require a soft HR strategy, and the choice of HR objectives and strategies will impact a business's financial performance. It will also affect the scale and resource mix used within the business and possibly its decisions regarding location. Finally, decisions in this area will have clear implications for the business's organisational structure and also employer–employee relations.

Developing and implementing workforce plans

Components of workforce plans

Businesses have to decide on the amount and type of labour that they will require, given their objectives and the anticipated level of sales. A workforce plan can detail:
- the number and type of workers required
- any redeployments
- redundancies
- retraining

An important element of a workforce plan is a skills audit to identify the abilities and qualities of the existing workforce, highlighting skills and talents of which managers were unaware.

A business's workforce plan will contain the following information:
- details of the current workforce — size, skills and locations
- an analysis of likely future changes in demand for the business's products and hence its labour needs
- an analysis of factors likely to affect the supply of labour, such as forecast rates of labour turnover for the business
- recommendations regarding the actions the firm needs to take to acquire and retain its desired workforce

Influences on workforce plans

There are a wide range of external and internal influences on workforce plans:
- **Sales forecasts.** Estimating sales for the next year or two can be a prime influence on workforce plans. This helps the business to identify the quantity and type of labour it will require.
- **Demographic trends.** These have a significant effect on potential entrants to the labour force. Migration is an example of one important factor.
- **Wage rates.** If wages are expected to rise, then businesses may reduce their demand for labour and look to replace it with more technology.
- **Technological developments.** Changes in technology may reduce the need for unskilled or even skilled employees.
- **Changes in legislation.** Employment laws can limit the number of hours employees may work each week or require businesses to offer employees benefits such as paternity leave.

Issues in workforce planning

- **Employer–employee relations.** A business should not take decisions about the workforce without consulting employees. Indeed, EU legislation makes this a legal requirement for larger businesses.
- **Changes in technology.** New technology offers businesses different ways to meet the needs of their customers. This may mean different numbers of employees are required, with different skills.
- **Migration.** In the early years of the twenty-first century, large numbers of economic migrants came from Eastern Europe to the UK, providing British businesses with a substantial source of relatively cheap labour.

Value of workforce planning

A number of factors need to be taken into account:
- Workforce planning enables managers to have the right employees available in the right place with the right skills. This gives a business a greater chance of meeting the needs of its customers and winning repeat orders.
- Planning in any function within a business encourages managers to look forward, assess likely changes and prepare considered responses. HR is no different from any other function within the business.

Examiner tip

Many students are vague about the contents of a workforce plan and unable to write good-quality analytical and evaluative answers in response. Ensure that you master this area of the specification when revising.

Knowledge check 31

What actions might a business take to change its actual workforce to match that set out in its workforce plan?

- Businesses operating in markets that are subject to wide fluctuations in costs, prices or demand might find it difficult to assess the volume and value of products that they expect to sell, and therefore to determine the quantity and types of labour that they require.

Analysis

Opportunities for analysis exist in the following areas:
- Explaining reasons why a business might have constructed a specific workforce plan.
- Examining the major issues a business may encounter when drawing up and implementing a workforce plan.
- Explaining the links between the workforce plan and other functional strategies.

Evaluation

A number of evaluative themes may be explored, including the following:
- Assessing the most important influences on a business's workforce plan.
- Judging the value to a business of using a workforce plan.

Links

Workforce planning requires the HR function to cooperate with other functions within a business. The plan must fit with the business's financial plans and its chosen financial strategy. It must also reflect the business's operational objectives. For example, if elements of lean production are to be introduced, training or recruitment may be required. Finally, the workforce plan must dovetail with the business's marketing objectives and strategy. Thus, if a strategy of diversification is selected, the workforce plan must support this by providing suitable employees.

Competitive organisational structures

Possible organisational structures

Functional structures

A **functional structure** operates a series of separate departments under the leadership of a senior manager. Its advantages are:
- It allows the business to be coordinated from the top and to have a sense of overall direction.
- It provides clear lines of communication and authority for all employees.
- It lets specialists operate in particular areas, such as marketing and research and development.

The disadvantages include:

- Senior managers may become very remote as the business grows.
- Decision making may be slow because of long lines of communication.
- It provides little coordination and direction to those lower in the organisation.

Matrix structures

A matrix structure (see Figure 14) combines the traditional departments of a functional structure with project teams. Thus, a project or task team established to develop a new product might include engineers and design specialists as well as those with marketing and production skills. Each team member can end up with two line managers — their normal departmental manager as well as the manager of the project.

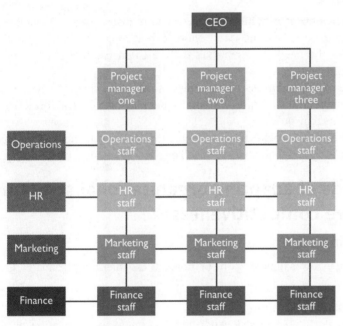

Figure 14 A matrix structure

The advantages are:

- It can help to break down traditional departmental barriers, improving communication across the entire organisation.
- It can allow individuals to use particular skills in a variety of contexts.
- It avoids the need for several departments to meet regularly, so reducing costs and improving coordination.

Its disadvantages include:

- Members of project teams may have divided loyalties, as they report to two or more line managers.
- There may not be a clear line of accountability for project teams, given the complex nature of matrix structures.

Other choices of structure

In addition, businesses may use two other organisational structures:

- **Entrepreneurial structures** are frequently found in small businesses operating in competitive markets. A few key workers at the core of the organisation — often the owner(s) — make the decisions.
- **Informal structures** exist where the organisation does not have an obvious structure. This is common in the case of professionals (doctors, for example), where they operate as a team.

Factors determining the choice of organisational structure

- **The environment in which the business is operating.** Competitive pressures may encourage delayering in an effort to reduce costs, while rapid change can emphasise the need for a matrix structure to ensure that the organisation can operate efficiently.
- **The size of the business can be important.** Many small businesses begin with an entrepreneurial structure, with the owner playing a central role, but change the structure as they grow.
- **The skills of the workforce.** The higher the level of skill the typical employee has, the more likely it is that businesses will organise along matrix or informal lines.

Knowledge check 33

Why do businesses with matrix structures often seek to recruit more skilled employees?

Methods of adapting organisational structures to improve competitiveness

Delayering

Delayering involves removing one or more levels of hierarchy from an organisational structure.

The advantages of delayering include:

- It offers opportunities for delegation, empowerment and motivation, as the number of managers is reduced and more authority is given to shop-floor workers.
- It can improve communication within the organisation, as messages have to pass through fewer levels of hierarchy.
- It can reduce costs, as fewer employees are required and employing middle managers can be expensive.

Delayering has some potential disadvantages:

- Not all organisations are suited to flatter organisational structures — mass production industries with low-skilled employees may not adapt easily.
- Delayering can have a negative impact on motivation due to job losses.
- Initial disruption may occur as people take on new responsibilities and fulfil new roles.

Knowledge check 34

In what ways might delayering improve the competitiveness of a business?

Use of flexible workforces

Flexible workforces are those that are adaptable to changing conditions and demands. A flexible workforce is likely to be multi-skilled, well trained and not resistant to change.

Flexible workforces can take a number of forms:

- Some of the workforce may be on part-time or temporary contracts, allowing the business to adapt smoothly to changes in the level of demand for its products.
- Employees may be on fixed short-term contracts. This is beneficial in that workers are not employed any longer than necessary.
- Employees may work flexible hours, through either flexitime or a system of annualised hours.
- Multi-skilled employees are an important element of a flexible workforce.

Delegation

Delegation can be defined as the passing of authority to a subordinate within an organisation — authority being the ability to carry out the task. However, although a task may be passed down from a superior to a subordinate, the senior manager still has the responsibility for making sure that the job is completed. In other words, it is possible to delegate authority, but responsibility remains with the delegator.

Trust is an important part of delegation, for both parties: the delegator must trust the delegatee to do the work, and the delegatee must feel sufficiently trusted to carry it out without interference. A prudent superior would also want to exercise some control over the subordinate — for example, via reports and inspections.

Centralisation and decentralisation

Centralisation occurs when most decisions are the responsibility of a few people at the top of an organisation. **Decentralisation** occurs when control has shifted horizontally (between people at the same level in the organisation), while delegation is a downward shift in control. Decentralisation is not the same as delegation but is often accompanied by it.

Decentralisation offers a range of benefits, in that it offers employees the prospect of greater independence in their working lives, known as **empowerment**, along with resulting motivational benefits. Disadvantages of centralisation are the training costs that might be incurred, as well as the loss of a common sense of direction throughout the organisation.

Analysis

Opportunities for analysis exist in the following areas:

- Examining the reasons why a business may have chosen a particular organisational structure.
- Explaining the HR methods a business may use to improve its degree of competitiveness.
- Discussing the advantages and disadvantages of the use of delayering, centralisation and decentralisation etc.

Evaluation

The following themes may require evaluation:

- Assessing the best way a business may adapt its organisational structure to improve its competitiveness.
- Judging the case for and against the use of flexible workforces.

Examiner tip
When tackling questions on flexible workforces, remember that they can be more valuable in industries where demand fluctuates or is seasonal and where demand is price elastic.

Examiner tip
Do define this word carefully: it is not the passing of responsibility but that of *authority* to subordinate employees.

Examiner tip
Make sure that you understand the difference between delegation and decentralisation as it is not unusual for students to confuse these two concepts.

Effective employer–employee relations

How employers manage communications with employees

Communication is the exchange of information between people within and outside organisations.

Employers use a number of communication techniques.

- **Meetings** can occur in a variety of forms, from formal meetings between groups representing employees to less formal discussions between individuals.
- **Presentations** are frequently used in businesses to explain policies and procedures to large groups of employees.
- **Technology** can be used by larger businesses to communicate with their employees. This can be of particular value to businesses that operate in several locations, especially if these are in different countries.

Communication can play an important part in motivating the workforce. Encouraging (and listening to) the views and opinions of all employees, perhaps through feedback, will increase their sense of self-worth and should improve motivation.

Effective internal communication can help to provide greater understanding of differences in cultures and opinions within an organisation. It may be the case that employees have different views on the business and its activities to those of managers.

Methods of employee representation

Trade unions

A **trade union** is an organised group of employees that aims to protect and enhance the economic position of its members. Trade unions offer a number of advantages to their members:

- negotiation of pay and conditions on their behalf (collective bargaining)
- protection from unsafe working practices
- a range of associated services, including financial and legal advice

Employers can also benefit from the existence of trade unions for the following reasons:

- They act as a communications link between management and employees.

- Professional negotiation on behalf of a large number of employees can save time and lessen the likelihood of disputes occurring.
- Trade unions are responsible for collective bargaining in the workplace. They negotiate with employers on behalf of their members on matters such as pay, conditions and fringe benefits.

Other methods of representation

Industrial democracy gives employees the means of influencing the decision-making processes within a business and a chance to represent their views to employers. Some businesses genuinely attempt to involve employees in decision making, while others implement relevant methods to improve public relations internally and externally.

The main methods of promoting industrial democracy are:
- Having **worker directors** — these are shop-floor representatives who are (usually) elected to be members of a business's board of directors.
- Setting up a works council, which provides a basis for regular meetings between representatives from management and employees. Works councils focus on ideas to improve the performance of the organisation at all levels.

Methods of avoiding and resolving industrial disputes

The improvement in industrial relations in recent years has, in part, been a consequence of two main techniques:
- **Arbitration** resolves a dispute by appointing an independent person or panel to decide upon a way of settling a dispute. Arbitration can take two main forms:
  - Non-binding arbitration, which involves a neutral third party making an award to settle a dispute that the parties concerned can accept or not.
  - Binding arbitration, which means that parties to the dispute have to take the award of the arbitrator.
- **Conciliation** is a method of resolving individual or collective disputes in which a neutral third party encourages the continuation of negotiation rather than industrial action. The conciliator's role does not involve making any judgement concerning the validity of either party's position.

Advisory, Conciliation and Arbitration Service (ACAS)

ACAS has the responsibility to prevent or resolve industrial disputes and provides employers and employees with arbitration and conciliation services. The organisation also offers other services:
- ACAS advises employers, trade unions and employers' associations on topics such as reducing absenteeism, employee sickness and payment systems.
- ACAS investigates individual cases of unfair discrimination and unfair dismissal.
- Initially, ACAS was principally involved in the resolution of industrial disputes. More recently, the organisation has focused on improving business practices to reduce the possibility of industrial disputes.

Examiner tip

Do not simply assume that a trade union damages the profitability of a business — it brings advantages and can help to control costs.

Knowledge check 36

What benefits might a business receive from appointing worker directors?

Knowledge check 37

What do you consider to be the major advantage of the use of binding arbitration?

Analysis

Opportunities for analysis exist in the following areas:

- Explaining how a business may communicate effectively with its employees.
- Examining the ways in which employees might be represented and the advantages and disadvantages of these approaches to employers and employees.

Evaluation

The following themes may require evaluation:

- Judging the best way to resolve an industrial dispute.
- Assessing the actions a business might take to avoid industrial disputes.

Links

There are obvious links with HR objectives and strategies, as well as with topics such as capital- and labour-intensive production. Employer–employee relations can also have implications for a business's financial performance and may be a non-financial factor influencing investment decisions.

Summary

- Human resource objectives are the targets pursued by the HR function of a business.
- The main HR objectives are matching the workforce's skills to the business's needs, using the workforce to its full potential and maintaining good employer–employee relations.
- There are a range of influences on a business's HR objectives. Internal influences will depend upon the type of products supplied by the business and the attitudes of senior managers. Employment legislation is likely to be a major external influence.
- Managers can use 'soft' or 'hard' HR strategies to achieve their HR objectives.
- A workforce plan details the number and type of workers required and how this is to be created. Sales forecasts, demographic trends and wage rates are factors that influence a workforce plan.
- Workforce planning can bring a range of benefits to a business, including encouraging managers to be forward-looking and allowing the business to meet customers' needs.
- There are a number of organisational structures that a business might deploy. Examples are functional, matrix, entrepreneurial and informal structures.
- Factors determining a business's choice of organisational structure are the environment in which it trades and the skills of its workforce.

- Businesses can adapt their organisational structures in a number of ways to improve their competitiveness. Delayering reduces costs by removing levels of hierarchy.
- Other adaptations are the use of delegation, the operation of flexible workforces and a policy of centralisation or decentralisation.
- Employing flexible workforces may involve the use of part-time or temporary contracts or annualised hours. Flexible workforces must respond well to changing conditions.
- Employers communicate with employees through meetings and presentations and increasingly through the use of information technology.
- A trade union is an organised group of employees that aims to protect and enhance the economic position of its members.
- Worker directors and works councils are other ways in which employees can influence decision making.
- Arbitration is the use of a third party to decide on a way of settling a dispute. Arbitration may be binding. Conciliation occurs when a neutral third party encourages the continuation of negotiations.
- The Advisory, Conciliation and Arbitration Service (ACAS) has the task of resolving or preventing industrial disputes.

Questions & Answers

In this section there are three case studies and associated questions. Each case study is accompanied by two sample answers, interspersed with examiner comments and advice on what the question requires.

A common problem for students when completing a topic is the lack of examination questions that cover only the topic in question. These questions, however, have been tailored so you can apply your knowledge and practise skills while topics are still relatively fresh in your mind. They are all focused on specific areas of content as covered in the Content Guidance section of this book. For example, the first case study is based on the finance section of the Unit 3 specification, although it also draws on your knowledge and understanding of AS business studies.

You can choose to tackle the questions either during the course or when you have completed your revision of that area of the specification. It is most helpful to use them to develop your examination technique, so allow yourself 1 hour and 45 minutes to read the case study and appendices carefully *and* to answer all parts of each question. Do spend plenty of time considering the materials you are given — the examination has been designed to allow you time to do this. Remember, you will always be given credit for using business concepts from outside Unit 3, provided their use is entirely relevant to the question.

By considering the specimen answers provided and the examiner comments, you will be able to see how these questions may be answered effectively and so avoid the potential pitfalls.

Sample answers

Resist the temptation to study the answers before you have attempted the questions. In each case, the first answer (by student A) is intended to show the type of response that would earn a grade A on that paper. An A grade does not mean perfection — these answers are intended to show the range of responses that can earn high marks. In business studies, it is the quality of reasoning that is rewarded. Student B's answers demonstrate responses that are worthy of a pass, but at a lower grade; the grade that would be awarded is shown in each case.

Examiner's comments

Comments on questions are preceded by the icon ⊜. They offer tips on what you need to do to gain full marks. Examiner's comments are also interspersed in the answers (preceded by the icon ⊜) and indicate the reasons for awarding marks. In the weaker answers, they also point out areas for improvement, specific problems and common errors.

Assessment

AS and A2 papers are designed to test certain skills. **Every mark that is awarded on an AS or an A2 paper is given for the demonstration of a skill.** The content of the specification (the theories, concepts and ideas) provides a framework to allow you to show your skills — recognising the content on its own is not enough to merit high marks.

The following skills are tested:
- **Knowledge and understanding** — recognising and describing business concepts and ideas.
- **Application** — being able to explain or apply your understanding to a variety of business scenarios.
- **Analysis** — developing a line of thought in order to demonstrate its causes, impact or consequences.
- **Evaluation** — making a judgement by weighing up the evidence provided.

The table below shows the weighting for skills for Units 3 and 4. As you can see, the balance of skills required varies between the two units.

Skill	Description	Weighting, Unit 3	Weighting, Unit 4
Knowledge	How well you know definitions, theories and ideas	20%	20%
Application	How well you can complete calculations and relate answers to the scenario	30%	20%
Analysis	How well you develop ideas and arguments and relate theory to circumstances	25%	25%
Evaluation	How well you judge the overall significance of the situation	25%	35%
Total		100%	100%

Skills requirement of a question

There are two guides to the skills requirement of a question. First, its mark allocation gives a rough indication of what is required. In the case of Unit 3, a total of 80 marks is available. For individual questions worth 18 marks, for example, the marks are awarded approximately as follows:
- **up to 4 marks** — a definition or description showing **knowledge**
- **a further 4 marks** — an explanation or calculation showing **application**
- **another 5 marks** — development of an argument in the context of the question showing **analysis**
- **a final 5 marks** — a judgement of a situation or proposed action demonstrating **evaluation**

These skills are awarded separately. If you write an evaluative response, therefore, it does not automatically mean that you will gain all the marks for the lower-level skills — so it is important to structure answers carefully to ensure that you demonstrate all the necessary skills. It is a good idea, for example, to start your answers by defining the key business term(s) in the question, as this is an excellent way to earn **knowledge** marks. Relating your answer to the scenario or carrying out calculations will be awarded **application** marks.

A more specific guide to the skills requirement of a question is to look at the trigger word within the question. **Specific trigger words will be used to show you when you are required to analyse or evaluate.** For A2 examination papers, these are usually the following:

Analyse

- 'Analyse...'
- 'Examine...'
- 'Explain why...'
- 'Why might...?'

Evaluate

- 'Evaluate...'
- 'Discuss...'
- 'To what extent...?'
- 'Assess...'
- 'Consider...'
- 'Comment upon...'
- 'Justify...'

All of the questions on AQA Unit 3 require analysis and/or evaluation, so these words will be commonplace and you should ensure that you understand what each one requires of you.

Students who fail to **analyse** generally do so because they have curtailed their argument. The words and phrases below serve to provide logical links in an argument:
- 'and so...'
- 'but in the long run...'
- 'which will mean/lead to...'
- 'because...'

By using them you can demonstrate your ability to analyse. Always ask yourself: 'Am I explaining *why*?'

In order to **evaluate**, you need to demonstrate judgement and the ability to reach a reasoned conclusion. The following terms will demonstrate to the examiner that this is your intention:
- 'The most significant...is...because...'
- 'However, ...would also need to be considered because...'
- 'The decision may depend upon...'
- 'The probable result is...because...'

Case study 1

Finance and accounts

Eastern adventure

A successful business

Flylo has been one of the UK's most successful low-cost airlines since its launch in 1990. The company, led by its controversial chief executive, Rhona Jackman, has enjoyed steadily rising sales and last year transported over 19 million passengers to 30 destinations throughout Europe. Rhona has stated on several occasions that the company's most important aim is growth. Despite the growth already achieved, Flylo remains a relatively small business and has to compete with substantially larger rivals. In some ways this puts the business at a financial disadvantage.

For the past 10 years the company has operated a simple business model, based on minimising its costs. This financial strategy has enabled the business to compete successfully with larger airlines such as British Airways and also other low-cost producers. Prior to the adoption of this strategy, the company was financially unsuccessful. Overall though, the company's share price has performed strongly and shareholders have been generally satisfied with dividend payouts.

However, the company's customers have complained about its policy of charging for a range of services, such as booking in baggage and for paying by credit card. Rhona Jackman is unconcerned by this and has proposed that the company charges customers £1 for using toilets on its planes.

The company's relations with its employees have also been somewhat unsettled. There have been a number of disputes regarding pay rates and Rhona Jackman's policy of making employees pay for their own uniforms and training has been universally unpopular. Despite this the company has had little trouble in recruiting new employees when necessary.

Over the last year the company has expanded and upgraded its fleet to meet possible environmental targets that the EU authorities may introduce in the near future. This has also helped the company to deflect some criticism of its operations that have appeared in the media.

The Asian project

At a recent meeting of the company's directors Rhona Jackman was very positive about Flylo's recent achievements. 'I thought the company performed well in 2010, but this was bettered by our 2011 performance,' she said. She went on to argue that the company must build on this success and outlined a plan to offer low-cost flights in Asia in a joint venture with an established (but relatively small) airline, Air Thailand.

The key elements of Rhona's plan are as follows:

- The joint venture will operate flights on 30 routes between major Asian cities such as Bangkok, Singapore, Manila and Hong Kong.
- Air Thailand will provide marketing support for the project and will give up some of its routes to help Flylo establish itself. For this Flylo will pay it 8% of its Asian revenues annually.
- The two companies have agreed to discuss the possibility of a full merger at some future date.
- In the longer term, Flylo hopes to negotiate an ability to operate flights into mainland China.
- Flylo will use its own planes, staff and brand image. It will be based in Bangkok, the capital of Thailand.

Rhona explained to the board that this project would cost an initial £400 million to set up, but that initial market research suggested that sales would rise strongly over the next few years. This was an attractive market, she explained, especially given that incomes in Europe are forecast to rise very slowly over the next few years.

Air Thailand was keen to secure this deal to improve its cash position, which has been weak for a number of years, and also to give it more power when negotiating with suppliers. Air Thailand has just appointed a new chief executive who is very ambitious and keen to develop the business that was established by his father 11 years ago.

Appendix A

Forecast cash flow for the Asian project

Year	Forecast net cash flows (£m)
2012	(400)
2013	52
2014	156
2015	190
2016	282

Relevant discounting factors (12%): year 1 — 0.89, year 2 — 0.79, year 3 — 0.71, year 4 — 0.64

Appendix B

Comparative industry data

Item	Flylo plc	Industry average
Labour turnover (last 5 years)	24.7%	16.9%
Average wage in 2011 (2009 = 100)	100	107
Average capacity utilisation on flights	91.35%	87.55%
ROCE (average of past 3 years)	18.75%	11.28%
Share price in 2011 (2008 = 100)	131	96
Complaints (per 1,000 passengers)	17.6	11.4

Appendix C

Accounts for Flylo plc (2010 and 2011)

Income statement items	2010	2011	Balance sheet items	2010	2011
	£m	£m		£m	£m
Revenue	906.4	879.8	Non-current (fixed) assets	811.3	909.6
Cost of sales	(471.4)	(440.7)			
Gross profit	435.0	439.1	Current assets	133.5	123.1
Overheads	(298.6)	(282.4)	Current liabilities	(150.1)	(170.8)
Operating profit	136.4	156.7	Non-current liabilities (long-term liabilities)	326.6	450.7
One-off items	34.3	(0.9)			
Profit before tax	170.7	155.8	Net assets	468.1	411.2
			Capital employed	794.7	861.9

Appendix D

Data relating to the Asian project

Forecast annual average rise in incomes in selected Asian countries over next 4 years	+7.2%
Average annual change in demand for air transport in Asia	+11.87%
Average income of Thai citizens	£3,950
Air Thailand return on capital, 2011	22.38%
Tax rate on company profits in Thailand (28% in the UK)	8.1%

Questions

> **(1) Use the average rate of return and the net present value method to calculate the forecast returns from the proposed entry to the Asian market for the first 4 years.**   (10 marks)

ⓔ This question requires you to complete two investment appraisal calculations. You should make sure that you show your workings and that you express the answer in the correct format. Remember that you may use your answers to this question when tackling question (4).

> **(2) To what extent do you agree with Flylo plc's decision to adopt a financial strategy of cost minimisation over recent years?**   (18 marks)

ⓔ You should address both sides of this question (i.e. fully develop arguments for and against this decision) and then state whether or not you agree with Flylo's decision and **justify** your decision.

> **(3) Do you agree with Rhona Jackman's assertion that Flylo plc's performance was better in 2011 than in 2010? You should use financial ratios to support your answer and justify your decision.**   (18 marks)

ⓔ This question requires a similar structure to question (2), which should be developed in substantial paragraphs.

> **(4) Using all the information available to you, complete the following tasks:**
> * **Analyse the case for Flylo plc's proposed expansion into the Asian market.**
> * **Analyse the case against Flylo plc's proposed expansion into the Asian market.**
> * **Make a justified recommendation on whether Flylo plc should go ahead with its strategy to enter the Asian market for cheap air travel.**   (34 marks)

ⓔ Use the case study and the appendices of data to answer this question. Follow the structure set out in the question — you may want to use headings for your three sections. Develop the two best arguments for and against the decision in the first two sections before making and supporting your judgement.

Student A

(1) The average rate of return is calculated by:

$$\frac{\text{average annual profit} \times 100}{\text{the cost of investment}}$$

In this case the total profit over 4 years = £52m + £156m + £190m + £282m – £400m

$$= \textbf{£280m}$$

The average annual profit = £280m/4 = £70m

So £70 million × 100/£400m = **17.5%**

Year	Net cash flow (£m)	Discounting factor	Present value (£m)
Now	(400)	1.00	(400.00)
1	52	0.89	46.28
2	156	0.79	123.24
3	190	0.71	134.90
4	282	0.64	180.48
Net present value			84.90

The net present value of the Asian project is positive, suggesting that the project is worthwhile financially, although this result may need to be compared with something.

ⓔ This is a good answer in many respects. The average rate of return calculation starts effectively with the stating of a correct formula and the subsequent workings are both correct and easy to follow. Although student A has not made an arithmetical error, the workings would be easy to follow if this had been the case. By using this effective piece of examination technique, this student has ensured that he will gain as many marks as possible.

Student A is also able to calculate the net present value of the Asian project accurately. The key strength of his answer is that the table he used guides him through the process correctly. He has also made some attempt to interpret his final figure for net present value. The question did not ask him to do so, but if you are asked to calculate figures such as this, it is important to be able to interpret them as they will almost certainly prove helpful when answering a later question. In this case, it would be useful as part of the evidence when answering question (4).

(2) A strategy of cost minimisation means that a business's managers seek to cut expenditure in all functional areas to the lowest level that allows an acceptable quality standard.

Flylo has received benefits from its decision to adopt a cost minimisation strategy. The text states that the company's profits have increased since this decision was taken and this has resulted in shareholders being highly satisfied with the company's financial performance. The company's return on capital is higher than the industry average — 18.75% as compared with 11.28% — and this gives the company a lot of advantages, for example allowing it to pay higher dividends to its shareholders. The value of the company has obviously increased quickly, giving shareholders a further benefit. Its share price has risen by 31% since 2008, while the average for the industry is a 4% fall. This performance makes it relatively easy for Flylo to sell more shares if necessary to raise capital for future expansion.

However, cost minimisation affects other parts of the business too and also other stakeholders. It is clear from Appendix B that the company's other stakeholders are less satisfied with the cost minimisation strategy. Customers are unhappy with extra charges that are added onto the price of a flight and complaints to the company are significantly higher than in the rest of the industry. Rhona Jackman should be worried about this but is not, and is planning further charges which may upset passengers. <u>Employees are also unhappy and the company's labour turnover figure is high at 24.7%, compared to 16.9% for the rest of the industry.</u> *Losing nearly a quarter of all employees each year can actually increase the company's costs through training and recruitment and Rhona Jackman should improve the way in which she treats employees if she wants to reduce the company's costs in the long run.*

So, is this cost minimisation strategy a good idea? Yes — in many ways it has been a big success. The company has been very successful over recent years and its passenger numbers have risen despite increasing customer complaints.

ⓔ There is much to admire in this answer. The structure is good and helps the student to address the demands of the question. He has chosen to use three main paragraphs, which is sensible in that it allows him to offer arguments on both sides of the question as well as an evaluative conclusion. I also like the brief opening paragraph, in which he defines a cost minimisation strategy to make certain that he has demonstrated relevant understanding. There are other strengths in this answer too. The student has made effective use of the data provided in the case study, especially those in Appendix B, which he has drawn on to develop arguments for and against the use of a financial strategy of cost minimisation (see underlined sentences). This allows the examiner to award marks for application and analysis.

There are aspects of this answer that could be improved, however. The most obvious shortcoming is the final paragraph. The student made a clear judgement and offered some support. However, this was not developed fully. One line of argument he could have considered was that only some stakeholder groups have been satisfied with this approach and that in the long run this could cause problems. In fact there is more thoughtful evaluation at the end of the previous paragraph (shown in italics).

(3) There is a lot of evidence to support Rhona Jackman's view that the company performed better in 2011 than in 2010. The value of the business expanded considerably, as the capital employed rose by over 8% from £794.7 million to £861.9 million. This represents a large rise in value and may be a reason why the business's share price has been so strong. Rhona's view is also supported by the most important measure of profitability, which is return on capital employed (ROCE). This is measured by dividing operating profit by the capital employed in the business and multiplying by 100 to express the answer as a percentage. The figures for the 2 years are:

2010   £136.4m × 100/£794.7m = 17.16%

2011   £156.7m × 100/£861.9m = 18.18%

<u>So this shows that the level of profit, taking into account the resources available to the business, has increased by about 1%. This is clear support for Rhona's view.</u> Added to this is the simple fact that the business made a better quality profit in 2011. Although the pre-tax profit was higher in 2010, much of this (£34.3m) comes from one-off items which are unlikely to happen again, making the profit low quality. The operating profit figure in 2011 was much higher and the company appeared to control its costs very well.

However, there are other figures too. The current ratio is very low in both years. This is calculated using the formula: current assets/current liabilities.

2010   133.5/150.1 = 0.89

2011   123.1/170.8 = 0.72

    These are very low figures and might mean that the company has difficulties in settling its debts. In 2011, the business has only 72 pence to pay each £1 of short-term debt. This is very worrying, given that it has borrowed more money and its non-current liabilities have increased a lot. However, it may be that an airline can run with low liquidity as passengers pay for flights before they take them and so the company is not waiting for cash inflows.

    Rhona may be right that the company's performance has improved. This appears to be the case financially. Although liquidity may be a problem, the level of profits has risen strongly at a time when a recession is taking place. This is impressive. *However, it is difficult to make a proper judgement about the company's overall performance as we do not have non-financial data. What has happened to its market share, for example?*

e This is a high-quality answer from student A. He obviously has good understanding of these aspects of the financial element of the Unit 3 specification. Once again he has structured his answer well and brought together good knowledge and effective examination skills.

    I like the fact that he has calculated only two ratios (no more were needed) and has interpreted the results fully (this aspect of his answer is underlined). The second example is particularly good quality. His choice of ratios was also good — ROCE is the critical ratio and this contrasts nicely with the current ratio. This was also a good choice in the sense that one set of results supports Rhona's view and the other opposes it.

    The evaluation at the end (shown in italics) is also good. He picks up on the wording of the question, which did not refer solely to finance, and this gives a clear and valuable line of judgement.

    The most important aspect of this answer is the planning that has gone into it. Student A has probably calculated more ratios than this answer reveals so as to be able to pick the 'best' two. Planning is indeed vital in responding to questions on this examination paper. He also has clearly thought about what the data in Appendix C are telling him. Hence, he is able to write a strong argument about profit quality. Overall, this is an impressive response.

(4) The case for the Asian project

There are several arguments in favour of this project. My answer to question (1) provided some evidence in support — the net present value over the first 4 years was over £84 million. This is a positive figure for the first years of this type of project, where Rhona admits that it will take some time to develop a decent share of the market. It can be seen that sales rise steadily across the 4-year period and that the rate seems to increase, suggesting that this is a good market to enter at this time.

    There are other factors supporting the judgement that the Asian air transport market is a good one. Incomes in selected Asian markets are forecast to rise strongly (at over 7.2%) and much faster than in Europe, which is the alternative market for Flylo. Demand for air travel is also rising quickly as distances in Asia are enormous and air travel is the best form of transport. An increase in demand of nearly 12% makes this an easier market to enter as there will be large numbers of new customers seeking an airline. Flylo's strategy of offering low-cost flights could be very appropriate in a market where consumers' incomes are rising to the level where they can afford this product. If it is successful, Flylo might be able to make these customers brand loyal and therefore generate future earnings.

The case against the Asian project

On the other hand there are problems with this project. The average rate of return on the Asian project is 17.5% — this is a little below what the company has achieved in its trading in 2011 as measured by Flylo's ROCE. This is not an encouraging figure for a project that could be risky: Flylo is entering a market in which it has no experience and limited knowledge, despite the links with Air Thailand.

Flylo plc has to raise £400 million to enter this market, which might prove difficult for a business that has already borrowed large sums of money. The company's non-current liabilities rose from £326.6 million in 2010 to £450.7 million in 2011. This is a large increase and has taken the company's gearing ratio to 52.29%. This is above the 50% yardstick that says that the business is highly geared. This means that a rise in interest rates may mean that Flylo is not able to pay the interest charges on these loans as they are due. The position is made worse by the company's poor liquidity. In 2009 Flylo's current ratio was 0.72, a figure which had fallen from the previous year. Finally this project involves a joint venture with Air Thailand — a company that has a weak cash position. Thus a lack of cash could threaten the entire project, especially in the early stages when sales are forecast to be relatively low.

Recommendations

This is a close judgement for the company. However, I would recommend that Flylo does enter the market for cheap air travel in Asia. Rhona Jackman is committed to growing Flylo plc as its major aim, and this project will help to achieve the target. The Asian market is set to expand and the growth and development of China will help. The data for average incomes in Asia are very encouraging, although they are for selected countries, so this may reduce the data's value. Demand for air travel is also rising quickly in Asia and this helps to support the decision. The risk is reduced by a joint venture with an established airline in Asia, especially in terms of marketing information.

The fact that costs are low in Asia (average Thai incomes are below £4,000) helps the decision and fits with the company's financial strategy. By keeping costs and prices low in this developing market, Flylo plc can enjoy a good share of a market that is growing quickly. This is a good opportunity and seems to be the right time to enter this particular market. Flylo's directors should go ahead with the Asian project.

ⓔ This final answer from student A is excellent. The question is a demanding one and he has shown good technique as well as good knowledge in his response. The technique is good in the sense that he has selected a relatively small number of arguments and has developed them fully and in context.

Using titles to follow the structure of the question and to ensure that he answered it fully was sensible. His answer was supported well by use of data and he linked together more than a single point in developing each argument. For example, when discussing Flylo's poor liquidity (see underlined portion of the text), he linked it to Air Thailand's weak cash position to make his argument stronger. This is very good examination technique.

Student A's recommendation was clearly stated at the outset and was well supported, drawing on key elements of his earlier analysis. This shows further evidence of this student's skills in planning answers and selecting the most relevant material. The final element of the evaluation (in italics) continues to support his decision, rather than weakening the judgement by offering the alternative view, as many students choose to do. This answer would have attracted high marks for evaluation.

ⓔ **This student has not just written an A-grade answer; he has produced a top A-grade response. His knowledge of relevant subject matter is exemplary. For instance, he developed a strong answer based on his thorough understanding of profit quality. He has also planned his answers to ensure he selected the best arguments and developed judgements which arose naturally from his earlier analysis. This has been supported by excellent examination technique. In particular his mastery of the skills of application and evaluation has been evident.**

Student B

(1) The average rate of return compares profits and the cost of the investment. This business's profits are £280 million.

So, the average rate of return is 280/400 = 70%.

The net present value is £52m × 0.89 + £156m × 0.79 + £190m × 0.71 + £282m × 0.64 = £46.28m + £138.84m + £134.90m + £180.48m = £500.50 million.

ⓔ The first part of student B's answer contains a fundamental error (280/400). She has not used the correct method as she has omitted to divide the total profits figure (£280m) by four (as there are 4 years in the financial forecast 2013–16) to arrive at the annual average figure for profits. Student B may have been helped by learning and writing down the relevant formula at the outset of her answer. This would have provided her with a template to follow when carrying out the average rate of return calculation and may have meant that she did not miss out on an important stage of it.

The second element of student B's answer is also incorrect on two counts. She has fallen into a common trap and has forgotten to deduct the initial cost of the investment in the Asian project as an initial stage of the calculation. She should have realised that an NPV of over £500 million on a 4-year project costing £400 million is very unlikely.

There is also a calculation error in this response. The student has used the wrong discounting factor when calculating the present value of year 2 (she put 138.84 instead of 123.24). An important point to note is that incorrect answers here will not be penalised again if the results are used in support of a later answer.

(2) The use of a financial strategy of cost minimisation is a good idea and Rhona Jackman is correct in making this decision. She has made Flylo plc a more successful business. The case study says that: **'This financial strategy has enabled the business to compete successfully with larger airlines such as British Airways and also other low-cost producers. Prior to the adoption of this strategy, the company was financially unsuccessful.'** So, the business did not make a lot of profits when it had a different financial strategy but the change has improved how the company operates and this has kept its shareholders happy. Shareholders are a very important stakeholder and without them a company cannot raise money for expansion, such as the Asian project.

But the company's employees are not happy with this strategy. They are paid less than workers in other airlines and pay is an important part of motivation. *Taylor said that it was the most important factor and that low pay would mean that employees were not highly motivated and productive.* Flylo's wages have not changed over 2 years from 2009 to 2011, while the wages of its competitors have risen from £100 to £107. This might mean that the company finds it difficult to recruit and keep the very best employees. *In a service business it is important to have top quality employees.*

On balance I think that the use of a financial strategy of cost minimisation is not a good idea for the business. This has resulted in employees being unhappy and customers are upset too and are likely to be more so in the future as Rhona Jackman is planning other unpopular moves. She needs to think about all groups who are part of the business. I think that she should change her mind and use a strategy of implementing profit centres.

e I feel that student B did not think about her answer carefully before starting it. She apparently did little, if any, planning. The Unit 3 examination gives you time to think about and plan answers to what are quite complex questions. In this case, student B began with a judgement which she had not really thought through. In the end, her final judgement was different (these two elements of her answer are underlined).

The other major weakness here was a failure to use the numerical material. The only figure she uses is the comparison of wages between Flylo and the rest of the industry. Even this contains an error as she does not understand the use of index numbers and has changed them to currency values. It is important to have a good understanding of the various ways in which data can be presented. In the second paragraph, she attempts to introduce theory (using F. W. Taylor) but does not develop her argument fully. This paragraph concludes with an excellent point about the importance of high-quality employees in a service industry, but this is not explored fully (both these elements of her answer are in italics).

This paragraph highlights a common error in poorly planned answers: too many points which are not developed. As a consequence, the student will not receive high marks for analysis. However, there are good aspects to this answer. She does attempt to address both sides of the question, she uses non-numerical information from the case — although it is not a good idea to include long quotes (shown in bold) — and she tries to reach a supported judgement.

(3) There are a number of ratios that can be calculated to judge Rhona's assertion. These are shown below.

	2010	2011
Gearing	41.10%	52.29%
Current ratio	0.89	0.72
Net profit margin	15.05%	17.18%
Asset turnover	1.97	2.14

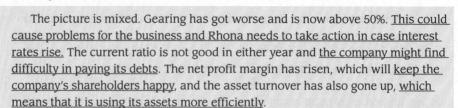

The picture is mixed. Gearing has got worse and is now above 50%. <u>This could cause problems for the business and Rhona needs to take action in case interest rates rise.</u> The current ratio is not good in either year and <u>the company might find difficulty in paying its debts.</u> The net profit margin has risen, which will <u>keep the company's shareholders happy</u>, and the asset turnover has also gone up, <u>which means that it is using its assets more efficiently</u>.

There is other evidence that can be used to support Rhona's view. The company has increased its capital, making it a more valuable business. In 2010 it was worth £794.7 million, but in 2011 its value has risen to £861.9 million. This is a big increase in value and <u>means that the company's shares will definitely be worth more</u>. The company's cost of sales and overheads were lower in 2011 too.

But in some ways 2010 was a better year. The most important argument is that its pre-tax profit was much higher in 2010. It was £170.7 million and it fell to £155.8 million in 2011. This is a big fall and profits are very important to public limited companies like this.

Overall I think that Rhona is probably right. Most of the ratios I have calculated support her view and the profit figure is higher in 2010 too. Although both years are good, 2010 is better in terms of both profits and liquidity.

ℯ Once again, student B has not thought her answer through carefully — there is no evidence of planning. A starting point should have been to consider which two or three ratios could be used most effectively to answer this question. She has opted to calculate four different ratios and has not shown her workings. In fact there are two errors here — can you find them?* Given this, it is surprising that she did not calculate ROCE, preferring to use net profit margin.

Her interpretation of the results of her financial ratios is limited. For example, she knows that a rise in gearing above 50% can be problematic and that this is linked to interest rate changes but she does not explain this fully. A higher mark for this argument would have been achieved if she had developed this answer fully. Much the same point can be made about the remainder of her answer to this question. There is a lot of evidence of incomplete analysis (underlined). She has been too ambitious in the number of arguments she has tried to develop. She has commented on most of the financial figures in Appendix C but has not developed any of these arguments fully. There is also some evidence of gaps in her knowledge as she does not comment on the large one-off item in the income statement in 2010.

The vague nature of her conclusion also limits the marks that can be awarded. The statement 'Most of the ratios I have calculated support her view' is too abstract. In fact, two of student B's ratios show improvement and two show a worsening. She is correct to state that liquidity is worsening but her conclusion that profits are better in 2010 is inconsistent with her calculation and suggests a misunderstanding of the need to focus on 'operating profit' in judging a company's performance. She also seems to reach a conclusion that is at odds with Rhona's, even though she says that 'Rhona is probably right'.

Nonetheless, there are strengths to this answer. The student does address the question directly throughout and makes a clear and supported attempt to make a judgement. It is a pity that she did not plan her answer carefully and focus on a smaller number of points allowing her to develop her answers fully, and that she did not check the consistency of her conclusion.

* The two errors are as follows:
  • For 2011, the net profit margin should be 17.81%, rather than 17.18%.
  • In 2010, the asset turnover should be 1.94, rather than 1.97.

(4) Flylo plc should agree to the Asian project. There are lots of reasons for this decision. <u>The sales of plane tickets in Asian countries are increasing quickly as incomes rise in those countries and as average incomes rise quickly too.</u> It is also encouraging that Air Thailand has a ROCE of 22.38%, which is higher than the average figure achieved by Flylo over the last 3 years.

<u>It should be cheap to set up a business in Thailand as costs will be low. Thai employees are not paid a high wage — £3,950 each per year which is about £75 a week.</u> This low cost for employees (important for an airline) will help to keep costs low.

The company will also benefit from setting up in Thailand because its costs of operation will be low and also <u>taxes on company profits are much lower than in the UK. This will give Flylo an extra 20% of any profits that it makes.</u> This will help to pay the money to Air Thailand.

If Flylo can operate in China it will help to make the company successful as China is a very large country and <u>a very large market with incomes that are going up quickly</u>. This could increase profits a lot in the future.

The chance of a merger with Air Thailand in the future should be attractive to Rhona Jackman as it will help her to expand her business if she controls the new business.

On the other hand there are a lot of risks involved in accepting the offer from Air Thailand. <u>Incomes are rising quickly in Asia but they are still very low.</u> How many flights each year can someone who earns an annual salary of £3,950 afford? Not many. So Flylo might be disappointed with its sales.

<u>Flylo has to pay 8% of its revenues to Air Thailand. This will reduce its profitability from this project.</u> Also how accurate is the market research for this project? The case study says that 'initial' market research has been conducted. Does this mean there is more to come? Will this give the same result? The financial forecasts might be wrong if this is wrong.

Can Flylo plc raise £400 million to pay for the Asian project? This is a large sum of money and may be beyond the company at the moment as its profits are falling. <u>Last year its profits fell from £170 million to £155 million, meaning that it will be difficult to pay for this from profits.</u> Can it borrow more money from the bank?

I would say that Flylo should choose the Asian project. The company's sales in Europe have fallen from £906 million to £879 million which means that it may not have growth over the next few years. In contrast the Asian market seems to be growing quickly and would be attractive to Flylo. This might prove to be a profitable and rapidly growing market.

e Student B's answer does not begin well. She says in her second sentence that there are 'lots of reasons' why the company should go ahead with the Asian project. This suggests that she is going to offer too many arguments and this is what she does. This is immediately evident from the large number of brief paragraphs that she uses. There are flashes of quality here, such as when she says that labour costs being low are important for an airline, but it is a shame that she did not develop this point in detail to say why this is the case. The structure of the answer, being many short paragraphs, indicates that she has not made her points fully. She has also developed a writing style where she asks a series of questions which are relevant, but then does not always answer them and thereby does not offer analysis.

However, there are many good aspects of this answer. Student B has identified many relevant points and has made some progress with them (these are underlined). It is interesting that most paragraphs contain good ideas, showing that it was this student's examination technique, rather than her knowledge, that let her down. She has considered both sides of the question and has offered a clear judgement with some support. This is a sound answer, but one that could easily be improved by more selective use of information, a fuller development of arguments and looking to link related points to make fuller arguments.

@ **This student had sound subject knowledge, although some gaps were noticeable. It was her examination technique that let her down rather than a lack of understanding. She would be advised to practise writing answers to this type of question to improve her examination skills and also to spend time thinking about and planning responses before she starts writing. Overall, this response would receive a grade C.**

Case study 2

Marketing

The 'anytime campaign'

Ashford plc is the UK's largest manufacturer of breakfast cereals. It supplies a range of well-known products under the single brand name and also supplies own-brand cereals for the UK's larger supermarkets such as Sainsbury's.

The company is long established and has grown significantly over the last 10 years, partly due to its expansion into the EU cereals market. The decision to sell products in the EU was taken in 2006 and has generated high levels of sales, with 31% of the company's revenue coming from this market. However, since 2009 sales have declined by about 5% as new competitors from the USA have emerged and new products with lower levels of salt and sugar have entered the market. The company has also spent heavily on adapting its existing products to meet the needs of diverse consumers across the EU and also on promoting products and the company's brand name. This increased costs significantly, especially in the short term.

Starting in late 2003, the company focused on increasing its sales revenue from the UK market through a strategy of market penetration. The marketing managers at Ashford plc have increased expenditure on all aspects of promotion and have agreed further deals with supermarkets to supply own-brand products for them. In October 2011, a £5 million marketing campaign was launched to promote some of the company's long-established products, including its luxury nut and cereal mix — Nature's Bounty. As part of the strategy of market penetration, the company has sought further outlets for its products and has negotiated a deal with BP to sell its products in garages throughout the UK.

Marketing manager Ravi Panesar is just putting the finishing touches to his proposal to sell the company's products in different markets within the UK. Ravi's proposal has the advantage of being relatively cheap to implement and may help the company to increase its sales further.

The main elements of Ravi's proposal are as follows.
- The company should target its products at consumers other than just its standard family shopper.
- The company's cereals should be packaged in different-sized boxes and in different ways (for example including milk, a plastic bowl and a spoon) to allow them to be 'fast' food.
- The company should put in place a major marketing campaign to sell its cereals as something to be eaten at any time of the day. Ravi calls this the 'anytime campaign'.
- The company should opt for premium prices for these products. Primary market research suggests that price elasticity of demand for these products will be –1.8.

- The company should seek to distribute its products in more outlets, including cafés, sports centres and pubs, as snack foods which are healthier than chocolate bars or crisps.

The 'anytime campaign' would not require the development of new products but simply the repackaging of existing products and presenting them in different ways to attract new groups of consumers. Ravi believes that levels of sugar and salt would not be major issues in this campaign.

Ravi has conducted extensive market research and this has resulted in positive findings. The company's main buyers are women aged 30–50, but primary research indicated that over 60% of the customers for the newly packaged and presented products would be young males aged between 18 and 35 who have high levels of disposable income. Ravi has been encouraged by the success of Kellogg's, who implemented a similar strategy in the UK several years ago and who has recently extended its range of this type of products.

However, some of Ravi's colleagues in the marketing department are less impressed by the potential of the 'anytime campaign', believing that it does not address the fundamental issues facing the company. The company will have to make a decision on whether to implement the 'anytime campaign'.

Appendix A

Correlation of UK promotional expenditure and UK sales revenue for Ashford plc 2001–2011

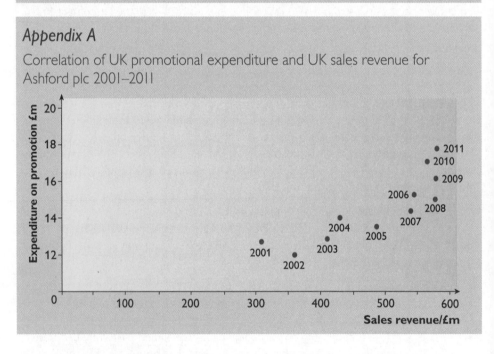

Appendix B

Comparative data on the UK and EU markets for cereals

	UK	EU (less UK)
Total annual expenditure on breakfast cereals by EU consumers (2011)	£1,717 million	£14,690 million
Average annual growth in expenditure on breakfast cereals (2006–10)	+0.15%	+1.9%
Estimated price elasticity of demand for breakfast cereals (2007)	−1.2	−0.9
Ashford plc's market share (2011)	34.5%	11.9%
Average net profit margin on Ashford plc's breakfast cereals	15.5%	8.7%

Appendix C

Marketing data for Ashford plc

	Ashford plc	Major competitors (average figures)
Average number of new products launched annually (2003–10)	3	22
Number of low-fat or low-salt products (2011)	5	13
Brand recognition by females aged 30–50	86.7%	39.9%
Brand recognition by males aged 18–35	22.4%	43.6%
Average price for a 300 g box of breakfast cereal (2007 = 100)	101	111

Appendix D

More data on the 'anytime campaign'

Total cost of marketing for the 'anytime campaign' (2013–15)	£14.1 million
Forecast net profit margin on 'anytime campaign' sales	26.7%
Forecast average annual growth of expenditure on 'anytime' products	+5.5%
Number of rival products available (2012)	33
Forecast number of similar products available (2014)	63
UK government average annual expenditure on 'healthy eating' (2012–15)	£15.5 million

Questions

(1) Examine the strengths and weaknesses of Appendix A for Ashford's plc's marketing department when analysing the UK market for breakfast cereals. (10 marks)

ⓔ It is important to address both sides of this question and to make sure you provide strengths and weaknesses in your answer. You should select and develop fully the best argument on either side of this question.

(2) Do you agree with the view that Ashford plc's move into the EU market was a good marketing decision? Justify your opinion. (18 marks)

ⓔ This is a typical 18-mark question from the BUSS3 paper in that it is two-sided and asks you to develop an argument on either side (as fully as possible and drawing on material from the case study) before making and supporting your judgement. The wording does not directly ask you to put arguments for and against, but it is impossible to make and fully support a judgement without doing this.

(3) To what extent do you support Ashford plc's decision to implement a UK strategy of market penetration? (18 marks)

ⓔ This question requires a similar approach to that of question (2) in that it calls for arguments for and against the strategy of market penetration and a supported judgement. However, you should note that question (2) asks you to consider the EU market whereas this one refers only to the UK market. It is essential to do exactly what the question requires of you.

(4) Using all the information available to you, complete the following tasks:
- **Analyse the case for Ashford plc's decision to implement its 'anytime campaign'.**
- **Analyse the case against Ashford plc's decision to implement its 'anytime campaign'.**
- **Make a justified recommendation on whether Ashford plc should go ahead with the decision to implement its 'anytime campaign'.** (34 marks)

ⓔ Use the case study and the appendices of data to answer this question. Follow the structure set out in the question — you may want to use headings for your three sections. Develop the two best arguments for and against the decision to adopt the 'anytime campaign' in the first two sections before making and supporting your judgement on whether the company should go ahead with this campaign.

Student A

(1) Appendix A shows the correlation between Ashford's promotional expenditure and its sales revenue. Correlation measures whether there is a relationship between two sets of values. A positive correlation means that they rise and fall together while a negative correlation shows that the value of one set of data rises while the value of the other set of data falls.

These data will not be of use to the company's marketing managers because they do not include anything on the EU, a market which is increasingly important for the company. This market is growing and the company will need marketing data to take the correct decision. The other problem with these data is that they look at promotional expenditure as a whole. This doesn't tell the company which of their aspects have been most useful in generating sales. For example, it might be helpful to know about in-store advertising as compared with television advertising. This would help to make decisions on how to spend the promotional budget in the future.

However, there is one very useful aspect of these data. *The company's managers should realise that spending more than about £15 million per annum on promotion in the UK does not appear to affect the company's sales very much. After 2008 the company increased spending from a little over £14 million to nearly £18 million with only a small effect on sales. This money was not well spent.* It may be that the company has high brand recognition or its products are seen as old fashioned and winning new customers is difficult. In any event, there is little point in spending more than this amount on promotion in the UK. The marketing budget could be spent on other things like developing new products.

e This is a good answer after a hesitant start. Initially student A spent some time defining and explaining correlation. The question did not really ask for this, certainly not in the detail she provided. Thereafter the quality of her answer improved markedly. Interestingly she chose to outline the weaknesses in the data and this was good, recognising that they only related to part of the company's market (this aspect of her answer is underlined). It is good examination technique to look at appendices such as this in the context of the business's operations.

Her assessment of the strengths of the data revealed that she had a good understanding of correlation and could apply it effectively to these circumstances (shown in italics). The key was to see that the data have a 'kink' in them and that spending more than £14–15 million on promotion in the UK appears to have little effect on sales. These data relate to several years of trading, giving them more reliability.

I also like the fact that she makes an attempt to link her answer to the notion of analysing the market, though perhaps this could have been done more fully, especially if she had settled for making fewer points. Indeed, one criticism is that this is a lengthy answer to a 10-mark question, which may limit the time available to the student to answer later questions, especially the final one.

(2) The EU market is much larger than the UK one and offers much more opportunity for the company to sell its products. Appendix B says that expenditure on breakfast products in the UK is £1,717 million compared with £14,690 million in the rest of the EU. This means that if the company only achieves a small

proportion of these sales, then it will earn large amounts of revenue. The fact that the company earns 31% of its revenue from this market is an indication of its importance and *that the decision was correct*. The EU also looks an attractive market in terms of prices. <u>Even though we do not know whether prices are actually higher there, the fact that demand is quite price inelastic is very useful for the company. The figure of −0.9 means that Ashford's marketing managers can increase prices without a huge loss of sales and that revenue will increase because of this.</u> *Price elasticity alone seems to make this a good marketing decision.*

One major drawback of the decision to enter this market is that the profit margin on sales in the EU is much lower, being under 9%. Although the company gets a lot of revenue from this market it may be that it does not receive much profit. The business has faced higher product costs in this market — for example transporting its products across Europe — and also higher promotion costs as it has established itself in the market. Also it has had to adapt its products to the demand of EU consumers. Profit is important for a public limited company. And more recently new competitors have appeared and sales have fallen by 5%. This could damage the company's profit margin further, *calling into question its decision to enter this market.*

Overall, this decision was a good one. The company has entered a large market where it seems to have more freedom in its pricing than in the UK. This market is growing at a time when sales in the UK seem to have stagnated — Appendix A shows that the company's UK sales have not altered much since 2007. **However, this will only prove to be a good marketing decision if the company's managers react appropriately to the new competition that has arrived. This will require further market analysis and the development of a new marketing plan to combat this threat.**

ⓔ This is a thoughtful and well-constructed response by student A. She has reacted appropriately to the wording of the question and has clearly considered the case for and against the company's decision to enter the European market. A pleasing feature of her answer is that she does not lose focus and regularly links her arguments to an assessment of the correctness of this particular marketing decision (shown in italics). This will be rewarded by marks for evaluation.

A further strength of her answer is the effective use she makes of the data given in the case study. An example of this is the strong argument that she builds based on the price elasticity of demand figure for the EU market. This shows excellent understanding of the relevant theory and is a good example of analytical writing (underlined). She might, however, have picked up on the fact that the data are estimated and relate to 2007 when the decision was made. Demand may now be more price elastic, especially as new competitors have entered this market.

Student A's evaluation is also good. She makes a clear judgement and supports it by selective reference to her earlier analysis and ongoing evaluation and to evidence from Appendix A. She deepens her evaluation by saying that this decision may only be a good one if the company responds to the changing market — this is good technique on her part and is shown in bold.

(3) Market penetration is a strategy designed to sell more of a business's existing products in its current market. Because the business is familiar with the market and the product, it is a low-risk strategy.

There are a number of reasons why Ashford plc was right to use this strategy in the UK. The company receives a higher profit margin on its UK sales than on those in Europe. The profit margin in the UK is nearly twice as high, at 15.5%. Therefore this means selling more in this market is more likely to have a bigger impact on its profits. This approach is also likely to involve less expenditure than other marketing strategies such as diversification, as this involves developing new products and analysing new markets. Both of these activities involve high costs and may not offer returns for many years, especially when operating together. Thus the strategy of market penetration will bring short-term profits which will please most of the company's shareholders and they are the most important stakeholder.

There are reasons against this strategy which the company's managers should have taken into account in their decision. The major one is that market penetration requires a reduction in price. This will eat away at the company's profit margin on each sale. There is evidence of this in Appendix C where the price charged by Ashford for its products has barely risen since 2007, while its competitors have enjoyed an 11% increase in revenue per unit over the same time. This will have weakened Ashford's competitive position, unless it has enjoyed a huge rise in sales volume. The price elasticity figure suggests that UK consumers will respond positively to price changes, so this might help the company and its use of this strategy.

This marketing strategy might work in the short run and maybe has done so, but Ashford plc cannot continue with it in the longer term if it is to remain competitive. *Its products are in danger of becoming outdated, as it is launching very few new ones and does not appear to be responding to the changing marketplace. Its future will depend on it opting for a strategy of product development whereby it responds to consumer demands for new low-fat and low-salt products.*

ⓔ This is another good answer by student A and could only have been written after careful planning. In the second paragraph, she makes reference to a 'major' argument, suggesting she had considered others but discarded them as part of her planning.

She starts sensibly by defining a strategy of market penetration fully and clearly. Thereafter she offers two effective paragraphs setting out the arguments in support of, and against, the use of this strategy. Her arguments are well constructed and bring together good lines of analysis (underlined), and using selective data from the case and appendices will ensure that she receives marks for application. This is obviously the result of careful planning and demonstrates excellent examination technique.

I particularly like her final paragraph, in which she offers high-quality evaluation (italicised). She looks at the bigger picture and makes a judgement, supported by some key data from Appendix C.

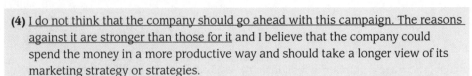
(4) <u>I do not think that the company should go ahead with this campaign. The reasons against it are stronger than those for it</u> and I believe that the company could spend the money in a more productive way and should take a longer view of its marketing strategy or strategies.

Ashford plc's position in the UK market is strong at the moment, although sales have been static for some years as shown in Appendix A. This means that the company does need to develop a new strategy to try and take the company forward in the UK market. In financial terms, this campaign does seem to be a good idea. *The profit margin that is forecast is 26.7% and this is much higher than what is achieved in either the standard UK or EU markets. As a business for which profits are important,* this is a key factor in the decision. *In addition the growth in expenditure in this particular market is forecast to be high, at 5.5%. This is attractive at a time when the major UK market for breakfast cereals is barely growing at all. Added to this is that the cost of the campaign is relatively low — only £14.1 million over 3 years.* Spending less than £5 million a year on this will not pose a financial problem for a company as large as Ashford plc, whose UK sales are nearly £600 million each year.

This campaign will also allow Ashford to sell its products to a new consumer group (young men) who have considerable amounts of disposable income to spend. Building up a brand identity with this group of consumers could assist the business in selling other products to them if new ones are developed in the near future. In this way the campaign has long-term potential.

But there are arguments against the anytime campaign too. This is not a new idea. The case study shows that a big competitor, Kellogg's, has sold this type of product for some time. So, although this is a growing market segment, there is well-known, established competition already present. This will make it more difficult for Ashford plc to break into the market and the company may have to spend more on marketing than it has forecast. *It is also worrying that there are already 33 products on the market and that another 30 are expected to be available by 2014. This means that although the market is growing, the number of rival products is growing more quickly.*

My major worry about this campaign is that the company is not really changing its products. It is simply repackaging them and presenting them in different ways. This doesn't take into account the changing demands of consumers and their desire to eat more healthily. Will even young men be willing to buy products that could be high in sugar and salt? The company is planning to spend less than £5 million each year promoting these new products, but the government is planning to spend three times as much on advertising the benefits of healthy eating.

On balance, I do not believe that Ravi's campaign is a good one for Ashford at the moment. Although it is cheap and easily affordable, it does not really take the business forward in the UK market in the long term. **Ashford plc needs to develop some new products. I would recommend that it abandons this campaign and develops new ranges of healthy low-sugar and low-salt foods and markets these to consumers in the UK and also in other parts of Europe**. The company could then consider selling these products in other markets such as the USA.

ⓔ Student A has followed the structure of the question in developing her answer — a sensible approach to tackling this type of strategic question in this examination. She did offer some evaluation at the outset (underlined) and this was not a problem given that she supported this view later in her answer.

Her response to the first element of the question was good. Once again, she uses the data effectively to develop her answer. She selects the data carefully (evidence of planning) and links them together well to develop a stronger argument (shown in italics). This constitutes good analysis. The second element of the question was answered equally well, again demonstrating good examination technique.

The final section is perhaps the least impressive part of this response. Student A makes an initial judgement and offers some material in support of this opinion. However, thereafter she drifts into a discussion of the marketing strategy that Ashford should adopt, rather than confining her discussion to the question in hand (this element of her answer is shown in bold). This is a common error, even among talented students such as student A, and one which should be avoided.

ⓔ **This is a very good set of responses to the questions on this paper and would receive an A grade. The student has excellent subject knowledge, bringing together material from the marketing element of the Unit 3 specification and that from AS business studies. Her examination skills are good. Generally she writes relevantly and has mastered the skills of application, analysis and evaluation.**

Student B

(1) The chart in Appendix A is very useful to Ashford's managers for a number of reasons. It tells the managers that when they spend more on promoting their products in the UK, sales rise. In 2001 the company spent about £13 million on advertising and this led to sales of about £300 million. This steadily increases until in 2011 the company spent about £18 million on promotion in the UK and achieved sales of just under £600 million. This tells the managers that it is worth spending more money on promotion in the UK. The chart also tells them something more. If the business spends more than about £14 million, the effect on sales does not seem to be so great. Since 2008 Ashford plc has increased its budget for promotional expenditure and its sales have not really changed very much. It might be that the company's managers should decide not to spend more than this amount of money on promotion in the UK in the future. Perhaps they should spend it in Europe.

ⓔ There are some good aspects to this answer. Student B starts slowly by explaining the positive correlation between expenditure on promotion and the company's sales revenue. However, he does pick out one key point — that the correlation breaks down after expenditure on promotion reaches £14–15 million. He makes this point clearly and considers its implications for the business. This strong analytical element of the answer (which is also applied well) is underlined.

However, there are some drawbacks to this answer. The student has really only answered half the question as he does not consider the weaknesses of the data when analysing markets. This is highlighted by the fact that he has written only a single paragraph. He needed to focus more directly both on what Appendix A tells Ashford plc's managers about the UK breakfast cereals market and on what it does not tell them.

(2) In some ways this was a good decision. Ashford plc has sold a lot of breakfast cereals in other EU countries and now has about 12% of this market. This means that the company receives about a third of its revenue from Europe, and if it can increase its market share more, this could become a more important market than the UK for the company. The EU market has total sales of nearly £15,000 million and Ashford has a good share of this. So in this way it was a good decision.

I think that it was also not a good decision. The company has faced higher costs because of this. <u>It has had to change its products because buyers in the EU want different cereals and they want different things too. This has meant higher costs and the company will not have made so much profit as it expected on sales in Europe.</u> The company has also had to spend a lot on promotion in Europe. *However, any big marketing decision is likely to involve high costs and this one is not unusual.*

It is always difficult to enter a new market and it is important to carry out plenty of market research before making any major decision. This is the analysis stage of the decision-making process. The next stage is the decision about the marketing strategy that is to be used. This could be market or product development. These are both considered to be medium risk. The final stage of the process is the writing of a marketing plan. This states the budget and includes the marketing objectives and how these are to be achieved. If Ashford's marketing managers went through this, then this was more likely to be a good decision.

In evaluation I think that this was a good marketing decision by Ashford plc despite the recent fall in sales. It is making the company a lot of revenue and this revenue is likely to grow more in the future.

ⓔ There are some good elements in student B's response. He sees the two sides of the argument and makes a number of valid points. However, he does not make the most of these arguments (some undeveloped elements of this answer are underlined) and makes little use of the numerical information in the appendices. No reference is made to market growth or to price elasticity. This may indicate limitations in subject knowledge. Good answers to this type of question normally rely on a mix of numerical and non-numerical information.

He also fails to explore the links in the data. For example, in his second paragraph his argument about profit could have been reinforced by reference to the profit margin figures in Appendix B. However, the final comment in that paragraph (shown in italics) is thoughtful and evaluative.

Unfortunately the third paragraph is mainly irrelevant. It contains some good points and evidence of understanding of marketing, but does not address the question. It is only in the final sentence that student B appears to remember the question and the context.

The final paragraph does offer some evaluation and a limited attempt at justification. This aspect of the answer required more development, which would have been possible if time had not been used up in writing the irrelevant paragraph.

(3) Market penetration means that a business's marketing strategy is to sell more of its products to its existing customers. Ansoff says that this is a low-risk strategy because nothing is new. <u>This is a good strategy for the company because it is spending a lot of money on its European marketing and this means that the business can cut its costs in the UK.</u> This will help it to make a larger profit overall. The company's strategy has been successful because it has agreed a deal with the oil company BP to sell its cereals in its garages in the UK. BP is a large company and has a lot of garages, and this could mean that the company will reach a lot of new customers and will receive a lot of revenue and profits from this deal. Ashford has also agreed further deals with supermarkets such as Sainsbury's to supply them with own-brand products. This is another major source of sales for the company, as supermarkets attract a lot of customers. If Ashford has more of its products on their shelves this is another reason why revenue and profits should rise.

But there are disadvantages to this strategy too. It has been quite expensive — the company has spent £5 million on a major UK marketing campaign which does not appear to have had much effect on its sales in Appendix A, although <u>this may need more time to have an effect on sales</u> as it did not start until late 2011. The company is going to have to win customers from other businesses if it is to increase its UK sales by a large percentage. Appendix B tells us that the UK market for breakfast cereals is barely growing. So, Ashford plc can only sell more products if its competitors sell smaller amounts. <u>This is difficult to achieve</u> as its competitors are bound to cut their prices or spend more on advertising or both. Also Ashford's competitors are developing lots of new products which might threaten the company's marketing strategy of market penetration.

ⓔ The weakness of this answer is apparent from looking at its structure. There are only two paragraphs, suggesting that student B has not offered a lot of evaluation in addition to considering the two sides of the argument. This is in fact the case. There is some judgement in these two paragraphs (underlined), but the question directly called for a clear and supported overall judgement, which was not provided.

The first paragraph is a bit disappointing in that it takes some time to set out two very similar arguments. These could have been combined and the student could have used the time to offer evaluation. The second paragraph contained some good points and it was obvious that student B had made use of selected information to assemble stronger arguments which were set in the context of the case study. This paragraph contained some judgements but it is a pity that he did not make an overall judgement in a final paragraph.

(4) For

There are many reasons why Ashford plc should implement the 'anytime campaign'. The company can introduce this quite quickly (which is not always true of marketing strategies) and this means that it could be a quick source of extra revenue for the company. This will help it at a time when sales in the EU are falling by 5% and when it has not been able to increase its sales revenue in the UK since 2008 despite spending a lot more on promotional activities. The campaign

will also have the chance to sell its products at premium prices. This means that it can sell at higher prices and that this will give it a higher profit margin. Appendix D tells us that this will be 26.7% which is much higher than anything else the company earns. So if it can sell a lot of products it will make a large amount of profits. This is a major reason why the company should go ahead with this idea.

Against

The big problem with Ravi's idea is that it is not a new one. We are told that Kellogg's has been doing the same thing for some time and this means that Ashford's market research might not be completely accurate in terms of profit margins. *Surely Kellogg's will cut its prices for this type of product if it sees that it faces serious competition from a company as big as Ashford plc? This means that Ashford will have to sell at lower prices to be able to compete in this market and that the amount of profit earned on each sale will be lower than is forecast.*

Also there are lots of rival products on the market even at the time that Ravi is planning his campaign. There are 33. Also other companies (or maybe Kellogg's) are planning to introduce more, meaning that there will be over 60 by 2014. This will make it difficult for Ashford plc to hit its sales targets, even if the market is forecast to grow by over 5% each year.

Decision

I would go ahead with this campaign as it is a short-term one and should bring in additional revenue without the company having to spend a huge amount of money to achieve its targets. Other companies that have implemented similar strategies have been successful and the growth in the market means that there should be room for more businesses in this market. Much depends on the accuracy of Ravi's market research, but he has carried out primary research so this is more likely to be accurate. Yes, I would go ahead with the 'anytime campaign'.

ⓔ This is a fair answer by student B. It is relevant throughout and addresses the requirements of the question. The student has used a range of numerical and non-numerical information from the case study to construct arguments for and against the implementation of this campaign. He has also reached a clear judgement (which is underlined) and has offered some evidence in support of his view, as well as commenting on the importance of the accuracy of marketing data in making marketing decisions.

The downsides of the answer are that it is relatively brief, given the time available to plan and write it. Furthermore the student has not always selected the most important data or used all available data when developing an argument. An example of this is that he discussed premium pricing without mentioning the figure for price elasticity of demand and using this to extend his analysis further (this part of the answer is in italics).

ⓔ **The student appreciated the skills that were needed to answer these questions and offered evidence of being able to provide most of them. His major shortcomings were gaps in his knowledge (sometimes relating to AS material) and his failure to combine information from the case study as well as from the appendices to build more powerful arguments. This answer is of grade-C standard.**

Case study 3

Human resources and operations management

Cosmetic changes

Wasim Akbar was adamant: 'We cannot stay as we are. The world is changing and we must change with it if we are to survive. Our competitors are driving their costs down and we must respond.'

The recently appointed chief executive's challenge brought about a moment of quiet in what had been a stormy board meeting for Natura Products plc. The company is the leading supplier of natural cosmetic products to UK retailers. Taking a strong environmental and ethical stance at its formation in 1990, Natura is in tune with consumers' demands for products that are not tested on animals and do not exploit people or the environment in the third world. Spectacular growth and lucrative contracts with high-street retailers such as Boots, Debenhams and John Lewis followed its establishment. Demand often soared (sometimes to unexpected levels) for the company's latest natural cosmetics.

However, over the last few years, profit margins have fallen, along with sales volumes. Last year's profit figure was only £150 million and 25% below forecasts. As a result the company's share price has declined.

A creative workforce and an innovative company

This situation was very different from that of just a few years ago. At that time Wasim's 'soft' human resource strategy was highly effective. The company's workforce was highly productive and creative through the use of kaizen groups and a flat organisational structure. The workforce was an important element of Wasim's innovative strategy. Many employees offered ideas for new products and supported Wasim and the management team in turning these ideas into reality.

Natura has developed a reputation for developing new products, often sourced from plants in remote areas of the globe. Despite a number of claims to the contrary by newspaper and television reporters, the company argues that developing new products does not harm the environment. This debate continues.

The company has also been at the forefront of developing natural recyclable containers from materials such as corn starch. This, along with its innovative products, has allowed Natura to charge premium prices for its products.

It was an obvious move for Natura to use techniques of lean production from the outset as these fitted in with the company's philosophy. The company has engaged in JIT production to support its use of kaizen at all levels of the workforce. It has a

'core' of suppliers with whom it has traded for many years, but has supplemented these with other businesses to reduce the risk associated with this approach to production.

A move to Poland?

Wasim surprised the board of directors with a proposal to move 80% of the company's production to Poland. The key features of his plan were as follows.

- The factories in Gloucester and Norwich to be closed and Natura's production in Barnsley scaled down.
- Workers to be redeployed wherever possible to other UK factories or offered voluntary redundancy packages.
- An estimated 1,200 compulsory redundancies will be necessary.
- Negotiations are complete to purchase a large factory in western Poland. This has the capacity to supply customers in the UK and provide an opportunity to break into the prosperous EU markets.
- Natura's product range is inadequate for the European market. To overcome this, £43.4 million has been included in the budget for the next 2 financial years to fund the necessary research and development.
- Market research suggests that sales to other EU countries could account for 45% of the company's revenue and 25% of its profits within 6 years.

There was considerable opposition to Wasim's plans from the other directors. One worker director commented: 'We have over 6,000 employees who are members of a trade union. If this goes ahead, industrial action is inevitable.' Another said that the company's profit margin was down to 4% and that this proposal would reduce this further, at least in the short term.

Appendix A

HR data for Natura Products plc

	Natura Products plc	Industry average
Labour turnover (2011)	2.1%	9.4%
Average span of control	14	7
Productivity in 2011 (2007 = 100)	124	109
Average annual expenditure on training per employee (2011)	£244	£137
Percentage of workforce that is temporary or part-time	3.2	37.1
Average cost of one compulsory redundancy	£6,900	N/A

Natura Products has been voted one of the UK's top five 'best businesses to work for' each year since 2003.

Appendix B

Natura Products plc's operations and marketing

- an average of 12 new products developed each year since 2002
- total expenditure on research into new packaging (2009–11): £17.1 million
- average annual expenditure to develop new products (2003–11): £54.9 million
- number of operational patents currently held by the company: 76
- Natura's prices are an average of 13% higher than those of its competitors

Average inventories (stocks) held by Natura Products (as a percentage of industry average)	16.5%
Number of suppliers used by Natura Products in 2011 (2005 = 100)	170
Number of products produced by Natura Products in 2011	92
Average price paid for supplies (as a percentage of industry average)	114%

Appendix C

Cost and other data for the relocation to Poland

Labour costs per hour (as a percentage of UK equivalent rate)	31.25%
Cost of transporting one lorry-load of products from Poland to UK	£2,852
Polish tax rate on company profits (UK rate: 28%)	16%
Percentage of Polish workforce speaking English	11%
Number of European suppliers that would be required	68
Estimated net cost of relocation to Poland	£322 million
Natura Products plc's gearing ratio prior to relocation proposal	48.5%

Questions

(1) Explain why Wasim might have originally decided to introduce a 'soft' HR strategy into the company's factories.

(10 marks)

ⓔ The words 'explain why' require you to write analytically in response to this question. When tackling this type of question, it is best to offer two arguments in separate paragraphs and to make sure that you apply your arguments to the scenario set out in the case study.

(2) Discuss whether the benefits of Natura Products plc's operational strategy of innovation outweighed its risks.

(18 marks)

ⓔ The command word 'discuss' clearly calls for evaluation and this is best answered using a three-paragraph structure. You should offer a strong argument on the benefits to this company of an innovation strategy and a strong argument against it. The final paragraph should contain a clear decision and supporting justification.

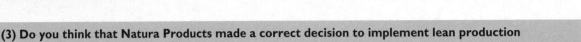

(3) Do you think that Natura Products made a correct decision to implement lean production techniques? Justify your decision. (18 marks)

ⓔ This question requires an answer with a similar structure to that deployed in response to question (2). Despite the wording of the question, you must explore both sides in your analysis to enable you to provide a fully reasoned justification.

(4) Using all the information available to you, complete the following tasks:

- **Analyse the case for Natura Products plc's proposed relocation to Poland.**
- **Analyse the case against Natura Products plc's proposed relocation to Poland.**
- **Make a justified recommendation on whether or not Natura Products plc should relocate to Poland.** (34 marks)

ⓔ Use the case study and the appendices of data to answer this question. You should follow the structure set out in the question — you may want to use these as headings for your three sections. Develop the two best arguments for and against the decision to relocate to Poland in the first two sections before making and supporting your judgement on whether the company should move to Poland or not.

Student A

(1) A 'soft' human resource strategy means that the business thinks that employees are important and it wants to train them and have long-term relationship with them. It is not a 'hire and fire' strategy.

Appendix A shows that Natura plc's workforce is very productive and performs well. This might in some ways be due to the way in which it is managed and the HR strategy that Wasim uses in the factories. Other factors will have affected this too, but the HR strategy is bound to have played a part. A key point is that Natura's rate of labour turnover *is far below that of other firms in the industry. It is only 2.1% whereas other firms have a rate of nearly 10%.* This offers Natura a number of interrelated benefits. The company does not have to pay to recruit and train large numbers of employees on a regular basis. This helps the company to keep its costs low for a number of reasons. Apart from the direct expense of recruiting and training, employees are likely to be more productive if they are experienced and this is shown by the *relatively rapid growth in productivity in the company's factories compared with other businesses in the same industry.* What is more, the company can gain more benefit from its kaizen scheme if its employees are experienced and therefore more able to offer valuable suggestions on how to improve the company's performance.

When the company does have to recruit employees, maybe because of its growth, it will be easier to attract high-quality employees because of its reputation as a 'good' employer. This means its new employees are likely to be more committed and productive.

ⓔ After starting with a definition of a 'soft' HR strategy, student A develops her answer rather slowly. The start of the next sentence is wordy and takes some time to get to the point. Once it does, she makes some very effective arguments and the best of her analysis is underlined. This slow progress indicates that it is unlikely that she planned her answers before starting writing. She was thinking about it while writing and this is not a good use of time.

One of the strengths of her answer is that she links separate pieces of data (shown in italics) to create a very powerful case for the use of a soft HR strategy and sets this fully in the context of Natura Products plc. This is a good answer.

---

(2) Innovation turns a new idea into a product that can be sold successfully. Natura Products plc has <u>benefited</u> from its strategy of innovation in that *it has a unique selling point and the possibility of charging higher prices than its competitors. We are told that the company charges prices about 13% higher than other companies in the market and this allows it to have a higher profit margin.* **This might be important** *as it is likely that Natura's prices are higher than its competitors because it spends more on training to make its employees more creative and innovative.* **The company has <u>also benefited</u> from innovation** as it has 76 patents in operation as a result of its innovative policies. This means that other companies cannot copy these ideas, although they might be allowed to produce them if they pay Natura a fee. In all these ways the company's innovative strategy benefits Natura by increasing the amount of revenue that it earns.

However, this approach does pose a risk for the company in a number of ways. Natura is <u>at risk</u> through the possibility of bad publicity about the way in which its production has harmed the environment. **This represents a big risk to Natura** because it has a USP based on its ethical and environmental policies. This has allowed the company to charge high prices and to gain high sales of its unique products. If its reputation is damaged, then it may lose sales and its ability to charge premium prices. This is a problem for Natura as it has very high fixed and variable costs to cover. A loss of reputation could lead to even lower levels of profitability at a time when this is already a problem for the company. **This means <u>the risk</u> is higher than it may have been in the past.**

Do the benefits outweigh the risks? Possibly less now than in the past, as the company's profits have fallen, meaning that any loss of sales revenue could be very harmful.

ⓔ One of the strengths of student A's answer to this question is that she picks up on the precise words used in the question, which is a good technique (see underlined words). This question did not ask for a discussion of the advantages and disadvantages of a strategy of innovation — it called for a consideration of the benefits and risks, which is very different. This is precisely what student A did.

She has argued very strongly that there are benefits in terms of premium pricing and has placed this argument firmly in the context of Natura Products. This argument has been developed well (see italics) and will receive good marks for application and analysis. Similarly she has picked up on hooks in the text about a media debate concerning the true impact of Natura's products and processes on the environment. This is an interesting argument to pursue in the context of the case and the question, and she has done it well.

The weakness of the answer is the lack of evaluation in the final paragraph. This stops short, possibly because of concerns about time or maybe a lack of ideas. Although the preceding two paragraphs do contain some evaluation (shown in bold), this answer needed a fuller evaluative conclusion.

(3) Lean production is a means of production that uses less of all resources and is therefore more efficient. This method of production makes sense for any company and not just Natura because it can help to reduce costs of production and so increase profit margins. In Natura's case, lean production allows the company to reduce its costs in a number of ways. Firstly, the company only holds inventories which are 16.5% of those of its competitors. This reduces costs in several ways. The company does not need such a large warehouse or large numbers of staff to manage the process of warehousing. It also reduces the possibility of theft or of stock perishing, which might be a major problem for this company. Also because the company might suddenly see an unexpected increase in demand for a new product, JIT manufacturing means that it is not left with large quantities of products which are not popular any longer. For a company that faces high costs in other areas of its operations, this saving is particularly valuable.

There are potential problems for Natura with this approach to production, however. The company has a large number of products that it produces (over 90) and a large and increasing number of suppliers — more than most of its competitors. This makes the JIT system more complex to run and increases the likelihood of the company not having some supplies that it needs and being unable to supply one of its large customers such as Boots. This might occur because one of the company's employees fails to order what is required and this is quite possible given the wide span of control in this business. It would be easy for a manager with a heavy workload to make such an error. The loss of such a large contract would be a major concern even for a business as large as Natura Products.

It could be argued that this approach to production is not right for Natura because it is too risky. *The company has a relatively small number of large and powerful customers and operates in a market where large swings in demand can occur when new products are launched. These are difficult to predict and the company's workforce is mainly full time. Natura might find it very difficult to respond quickly to a sudden change in demand, which is likely to happen as it produces to order. I think the company should hold a significant buffer stock of its products even though this is more costly.*

ⓔ Student A continues to show good examination technique. This is evident in her first paragraph, where she links together a number of aspects of lean production and uses these as the basis for arguing that this approach to production lowers costs. She puts this nicely in context by considering the nature of the products, the nature of the market and also Natura's financial position. This is a highly competent piece of writing combining good application and analysis (underlined).

The remainder of this answer is also of high quality. The student has offered strong arguments and then an imaginative and supported judgement bringing together two pieces of evidence from the case study. This is a highly effective way of offering evaluation (see italics).

(4) The case for

Natura Product's profits have been declining for a number of years and have fallen faster than expected recently. **This is a major reason** for the company to go ahead with this proposal. <u>The move to Poland offers the company the chance to cut a lot of its costs and to increase its profit margin above its current 4% — which seems very low. Moving to Poland will allow the average cost of employing someone to fall by about two-thirds and savings in manufacturing labour costs could be high. The company will replace at least 1,200 workers,</u> **so over time this could represent a large saving.** Another very important aspect of the financial benefits of the move to Poland is that the company's tax bill is likely to fall by 12%. This means that the company will save £18 million each year based on last year's profits figure — and this was regarded as a very low figure.

The other major advantage of this move is the opportunity it provides to break into the large EU market. **This is obviously a large market with the potential to generate a lot of sales** and, being located in western Poland, the new factory will be near to the prosperous German markets. This is a very good location. Wasim has forecast that sales in Europe could account for 45% of the company's revenue within 6 years, though they are likely to generate a lower profit margin as profits will be a lower percentage.

The case against

There are also significant financial costs, especially in the short term, of this relocation to Poland. The company will have to pay for voluntary redundancies and also for compulsory ones. <u>The compulsory redundancies will cost Natura £8.28 million in redundancy payments as well as a range of other costs at a time when the company is not profitable and a share issue may be problematic. The entire cost of the relocation is estimated to be £322 million</u> (**and could easily be higher as such costs tend to increase over time**). <u>The company may have significant problems in raising this finance as its profits are low and it is already operating with a gearing ratio of 48.5%, which does not offer much opportunity to borrow further without becoming very vulnerable to a rise in interest rates,</u> even if a creditor can be found. Wasim's outline proposal does not really mention finance or suggest how this proposal will be funded.

There are other additional costs too. A large quantity of products will have to be transported from Poland to the UK to meet the needs of retailers and consumers. This will be expensive as the cost of transporting a single lorry between the two countries is nearly £3,000. But this is not simply a financial cost. There is a large environmental cost here too — this is a surprising move for a company that has a strong reputation for being ethical and environmentally friendly. Wasim might find it difficult to answer criticisms in the media if he goes ahead with this proposal.

The decision

In financial terms it could be argued that the short-term implications of this proposal are mainly negative. There is the issue of a huge investment to be made at a time when the company is not very profitable. This could be supplemented by a decline in sales if Natura's reputation is damaged by the move and this seems likely. The short-term costs could be added to by the high possibility of strike

action by the company's workforce, of whom 6,000 are members of a trade union. **In the longer term Natura's financial situation might improve if Wasim's forecasts about increasing sales from the EU come about at the same time as the costs of production fall because of the move to Poland. Of course, the forecasts might be wrong and for this reason I am doubtful about whether the company should make this move.**

Natura Products **is quite a distinctive company** and it has an excellent reputation as well as an effective way of managing its employees which brings the best out of them and has benefited the company in the long run. **It is well known for its ethical reputation and its concern for the environment. It supplies using just-in-time production methods in what must be a complex system. The relocation to Poland seems to abandon all these basic principles and will move the company away from its core market for the chance of higher sales in Europe. This is too great a risk and the company should not relocate to Poland.**

🅔 This is a well-planned and structured answer. Student A has clearly thought about this carefully before writing and has selected the best arguments to use on either side — that is, the ones that she can develop most fully and apply most effectively to the case study. This emphasises the importance of careful planning in achieving high marks on this paper.

A key strength of this answer is that student A is prepared to use a range of business studies theories in support of her answer, even though this case study focuses mainly on HR and operations management. She develops excellent points on each side of this decision, selecting just two in each case, giving herself time to develop them fully and to apply them carefully to Natura's circumstances. This is first-class examination technique and is rewarded by high marks for application and analysis (some examples are underlined).

Student A's conclusion is thoughtful and well focused. She steadily builds up her case for not going ahead with the decision, considering financial and operations elements before arriving at a considered and fully supported conclusion. She also offers evaluation throughout her answer (many examples of her evaluative writing are shown in bold). This is a very good answer.

🅔 **This set of answers is excellent. The student has no obvious weaknesses in terms of subject knowledge and her examination skills are excellent. She has managed her time well and has always written relevantly. She is deserving of a high grade A.**

Student B

(1) Wasim might have had a number of reasons for introducing a soft HR strategy to the company's factories. He might have wanted to give employees more power and control over their working lives in the hope that they would perform better. This type of soft strategy usually gives employees a greater say in decision making and this can help the business to get more out of its typical employees. The reason for this is that a soft HR strategy gives employees a more interesting job and empowers them to take decisions. This might make them more productive, helping the business to reduce its costs of production and also its prices. This can make the business more competitive.

A soft human resource strategy will also mean that the business's employees are more likely to be motivated. <u>For example, training employees can help to meet their ego and esteem needs according to Maslow. He said that if employees are well paid and their jobs are safe and secure, a method of motivating them further is to make them feel better about themselves at work.</u> Paying for training is a vote of confidence in the employee by the managers of the business. It makes the employee feel a valued part of the business and will encourage him or her to work harder. Training will also give the skills to make this possible. This is why Wasim introduced a soft human resource strategy to the company's factories.

(e) The first sentence of student B's answer is irrelevant as it is really a reorganisation of the question and is of no value as an answer. Thereafter the student gives some powerful arguments as to why Wasim might have taken this decision. These reflect a good understanding of relevant theory (both from AS and A2 studies) and these are argued well and linked together. Examples of these are underlined and they demonstrate good analysis.

However, there is a major weakness in this answer. Student B ignores the context entirely. Two mentions of Wasim's name are not sufficient to gain marks for application and she makes no other attempt to use any of the information from the case study in support of her use of theory. This is disappointing, given that Appendix A offered a wealth of evidence on which she could have drawn selectively.

(2) Innovation is coming up with many ideas for new products. Natura Products is good at doing this and has 76 patents on ideas that it has developed. This offers the company lots of advantages. Having a patent means that Natura can charge high prices to its customers for these products and no one else can copy the ideas. <u>Another important benefit</u> is that the company can sell the patent if it wants to and raise more money.

Other advantages of being innovative are that the company gets a lot of new products to launch. Appendix B says that Natura Products launches 12 new products each year. This gives the company a boost to its profits as these products cannot be sold by any other businesses.

But there are problems with this innovation strategy too. The company has to pay high costs to develop all these products and many of its ideas (on which it has spent money) will not work and will be a waste of money. Appendix B says that the company spends over £50 million a year on innovation and that it has spent another £30 million on developing environmentally-friendly packaging. <u>These figures add greatly</u> to the company's high costs.

<u>The benefits of this strategy of innovation are greater than the risks. This is because the company is in an industry where people want new products on a regular basis. If the company can produce new natural products that do not have chemicals and might help people to look younger, then it will sell a lot of these products and will be able to charge high prices and make a lot of money. This company has a special type of innovation, but I think that all companies in this industry would have to be innovative to survive.</u>

ⓔ This answer provides an interesting contrast to that given by student A. Student B has a less clear understanding of the term 'innovation' and initially suggests it is just coming up with ideas. She then drifts into an argument on patents without expressly linking this to innovation, as student A did.

Student B has some good ideas about the benefits and problems of a strategy of innovation. However, there are two weaknesses here. She does not develop her arguments fully. For example she says that the company invests heavily in innovation but does not go on to develop this point and say how this represents a real risk for the company in its current weak financial position. Also she does not directly address the issue of risk, therefore limiting the relevance of her answer and her ability to evaluate effectively.

A strength of this answer is the quality of student B's evaluation, which is underlined. She has used the nature of the industry as a basis for her judgement. This is a sensible approach and much of the best-quality evaluation is based on the skill of application. Overall this is an answer of mixed quality.

---

(3) Lean production means making less waste in manufacturing by using smaller amounts of resources more efficiently. *This is a good approach for the company* because it means that it does not have to hold many inventories, making its costs lower. This is important for Natura because it has a lot of different products (92) and this would mean that it would need a big and expensive warehouse to hold buffer stocks of all these products. It is also launching 12 new products every year, so this problem would become a lot worse as it will have over 100 products to hold in its warehouse next year. This helps the company to reduce its costs at a time when its profits are falling anyway. This way of producing will be popular with the company's shareholders. Arguments against include the idea that the company pays more for its supplies than the other businesses in the area. *So, is it really just transferring costs rather than reducing them?*

Overall, *I think that lean production is not a particularly good idea for Natura Products. The company is not really facing lower costs as it has to pay its suppliers more for its products and this probably offsets any financial advantages that the company gains from its savings in terms of not having a large warehouse full of 92 products and having to pay lots of people to look after it.*

ⓔ Student B made a good start to this answer by offering a concise and accurate definition of lean production. The first element contains some good ideas and shows that there is more than one way of interpreting data when compared with student A's answer. There is plenty of evidence of application here, examples of which are underlined. Student B does, however, appear to forget that the company may stop producing some of its products over the next year.

This first paragraph continues to include a significant disadvantage of this method of production, which student B uses to develop the remainder of her response. This is a good point which could have been explored more fully and possibly compared to the price premium that Natura Products is able to gain because of its reputation and its products. The evaluation is clear and supported (see italics) but really centres on the same point of having to pay higher costs to suppliers for operating a JIT system. There was a lot more that the student could have said to develop this further, such as the company's ability to respond to a sudden increase in demand.

(4) There are lots of reasons why Natura should take up Wasim's idea and move to Poland. The company will benefit in many ways from lower costs. These include:

- wage costs which are about 30% of those in Britain and the company employs many people
- tax rates which are much lower than in the UK
- other costs will be lower too — the factory will cost less money and fuel might be cheaper too
- redundancies are more expensive in the UK as well, I am sure

The company should also think about being in Europe as there are 400 million European consumers waiting to buy its products. Wasim reckons that sales could rise by 45% over the next few years, giving the company a major boost.

The company might eventually be able to shut down all its UK factories and move completely to Poland. This will reduce its costs even further and it might be able to increase its profits a long way above the £150 million that it made last year.

Already 11% of the Polish workforce speak English and this will make it easy to recruit workers who speak the language, making it much easier to manage them and to have high levels of productivity.

But there are arguments against too. The company will have to pay to transport a lot of its products from Poland to the UK and some of these might be damaged on the journey, especially when crossing the sea.

It will cost Natura Products £322 million for this entire relocation. This is more than the company's profits last year. Can the company really afford this move?

The company will have to find 68 new suppliers to deliver products to the company and this might be difficult. The suppliers may not speak fluent English.

I think that the company should move to Poland. As I said earlier, this opens up the whole EU market with millions of new consumers. When added to the UK ones that Natura already has, this could give the company the big increase in revenue and profits that it wants. Wasim is an ambitious and clever manager and the directors should accept his proposals.

e Student B's examination technique fell apart when answering this final question. She appeared to want to use every single fact included in the case study rather than selecting the ones that she felt were most important. Because she attempted to write about so many of the factors affecting the decision, she did little with any of them. Take, for example, her treatment of the cost of relocation (underlined). It was lightweight in the extreme. The sum of £322 million is enormous and this company may well have difficulty raising such an amount at this time. There is plenty in the case she could have drawn on to develop her argument (such as the gearing figure), but she did not do so. It is vital to put together different elements of the evidence to form stronger arguments when answering this type of question.

The recommendations (shown in italics) are also weak. They are simply a repetition of earlier arguments. A well-planned answer would have held back some key factors as well as taking an overview of the earlier analysis. It is important to compare this answer with that written by student A.

e This was a slightly mixed set of answers in terms of quality and would achieve a grade **D**. The student offered some fair answers earlier on (though at times she ignored the skill of evaluation). However, her weak answer to this final question will have had a significant impact on her overall grade as it carries a high proportion of the marks — over 40%.

1 An objective is a target pursued by a business, or a function of the business. An example of a marketing objective might be to increase market share.

A strategy is a medium- to long-term plan to achieve an objective. A strategy to increase market share might be the development of new products.

2 If the company achieves its ROCE target, it may be in a better position to pay its shareholders dividends and the share price may rise, offering the chance of a capital gain. This may only be true, however, if the ROCE target is judged to be relatively demanding.

3 a) Cash in the business's bank account = current asset; b) an overdraft = current liability; c) a 12-year bank loan = non-current liability; d) debts owed to a supplier = current liability; e) the business's property = non-current asset; f) goods made but not sold = current asset.

4 If a business has too little working capital, it may be unable to pay its bills as they become due and this can lead to the business having to cease trading. In contrast, holding too much working capital means that the business's assets are not being used effectively to generate profits.

5 A rise in depreciation will increase the business's expenses thereby reducing its profits (on paper at least).

6 It allows managers to see how often stock is sold. A high inventory turnover suggests a quicker inflow of cash, so this should help to improve a business's flow.

7 Profitability measures the extent to which revenues exceed costs over some time period. Profitability is normally measured in relation to something else, such as sales revenue or capital employed. Financial efficiency looks at specific elements of financial performance, such as how quickly debts are paid and how long it takes a company to sell its inventories.

8 The acid test ratio excludes inventories (stock), which can take time to sell and may not generate cash quickly enough to be available to settle its bills as they are due for payment.

9 The gearing ratio may be of value here. It can guide a business as to whether its borrowing is too great in relation to the overall capital employed.

10 If demand is price elastic, consumers' buying decisions are sensitive to price changes. Hence a reduction in costs enables a cut in price, which should result in a significant increase in sales, which is likely to boost profits.

11 Payback ignores the overall profit earned on an investment, while ARR does not take into account the timing of flows of income and payments.

12 Not necessarily. It depends on the relationship between risk and profit. If the potential profits are sufficiently attractive, then even a high-risk investment may be justifiable.

13 Market size measures the total sales recorded in an industry as a whole. Market share measures the proportion or percentage of total sales in a market that is achieved by a particular business or product.

14 They want to establish sales trends because by being able to forecast future sales, they can ensure that they have sufficient resources available. In effect, this can help management teams to manage capacity utilisation, thereby minimising costs while ensuring that demand is met.

15 In these circumstances, a business might enter different markets (market development), decide to sell different products (product development) or both (diversification).

16 It may not have a recognised brand name, it will have to develop distribution networks (if it is a good), it will need to organise retail outlets and it may face tough competition from established competitors. This decision will incur significant costs, not least for promotion purposes.

17 The financial returns from high-risk strategies can be attractive. If a strategy succeeds, it may be that high levels of sales (earning high profit margins) can be achieved, which may help a business to meet its profit objectives.

18 Market research may be inaccurate and sales may be different from forecasts. Competitors may react in unexpected ways (e.g. by reducing prices), affecting sales. The external environment may change unexpectedly — the economy may move into a recession (as in 2008).

19 Invention is the creation of a new product or process, while innovation is a broader term that involves bringing new products or processes onto the market. Thus innovation relates to the development of commercially viable new products or processes.

20 The existence of economies of scale will reduce average or unit costs as a business increases its level of output. Assuming that its prices remain unchanged, this will increase the firm's profit margins.

21 Such a business may find it difficult to replace employees with technology and may therefore opt not to become capital intensive.

22 The business may promote its product heavily as the original or emphasise its brand and its distinctiveness in an attempt to develop and strengthen brand loyalty. Alternatively, it may pursue a policy of continuous innovation to remain ahead of rivals.

23 Such businesses need warehouses to store and distribute their products. Cost will play a key role here and so relatively low-cost premises will be required as well as efficient transport services.

24 Decentralisation entails passing power from the head office to branches or parts of a business. This is a natural development with multi-site locations as it becomes more difficult for senior managers to take all decisions and more junior employees will be granted greater authority.

25 The business not only incurs heavy research and development costs, but also possibly promotion costs to inform consumers of new products. They may also suffer from 'me-too' products which may have lower prices as the businesses selling them will have incurred lower production costs.

26 Businesses using JIT will not require as much space to store raw materials and finished products. This will mean that fewer employees and less property will be needed. The business will not have resources tied up in unsold products as they are, in effect, made to order.

27 A business might invest in training its employees or implement a system of recruitment and selection designed to appoint workers with the skills that are required.

28 The key reason is that the business will benefit in terms of greater production and productivity. This should occur as workers use their skills more fully and become motivated as a consequence of carrying out more demanding roles.

29 Good employer–employee relations mean that the two parties communicate effectively and that any potential disputes are resolved before industrial action is taken.

30 Good employer–employee relations may mean that a business avoids negative publicity concerning industrial action such as strikes. It should also mean that the business is more likely to maintain a continuous supply of products to its customers.

31 The business might make some employees redundant or redeploy others to different parts of the business. It may also train existing employees to provide them with the necessary skills, or it may recruit new employees.

32 A functional structure is based on a series of departments such as marketing and can end up with many levels of hierarchy and ultimately slow communication. A matrix structure is flexible and designed to enable businesses to solve problems and take decisions. However, employees can have several leaders.

33 In matrix structures, it is not unusual for employees to be given greater authority to take decisions and solve problems as part of one or more teams. It is vital that all employees have the necessary skills to carry out these job roles.

34 A major way is through a substantial reduction in long-term wage costs as many firms make middle managers redundant when delayering. This can cut overall costs and improve price competitiveness. A flatter structure may also be more responsive to changes in customers' needs.

35 Technology allows global businesses to have immediate communication using e-mail and therefore speeding up decision making. It also enables the rapid transfer of designs to manufacturing centres in Asia, reducing delays in production for multinational businesses.

36 Benefits might include having particular expertise (and a different perspective) on the board of directors, improving the quality of decisions. Also this may improve the motivation and performance of employees if they feel that their views are represented at this level.

37 This type of arbitration is certain to deliver a resolution that will be accepted by both sides, thereby ending the dispute.

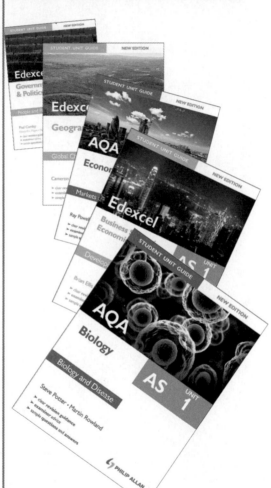

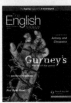
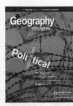
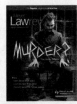